BEI...

LOVE

WISDOM

TRUTH

Copyright © translation by Darin Stoytchev
ISBN 978 1461060987
E-mail address: mainpem@gmail.com

To receive this book together with the books "The Might ofLove", and "Prayers and Spiritual Formulas" for free (digital format) send an email to: mainpem@gmail.com

Printed in Santa Monica CA U.S.A
Copyright © 2011

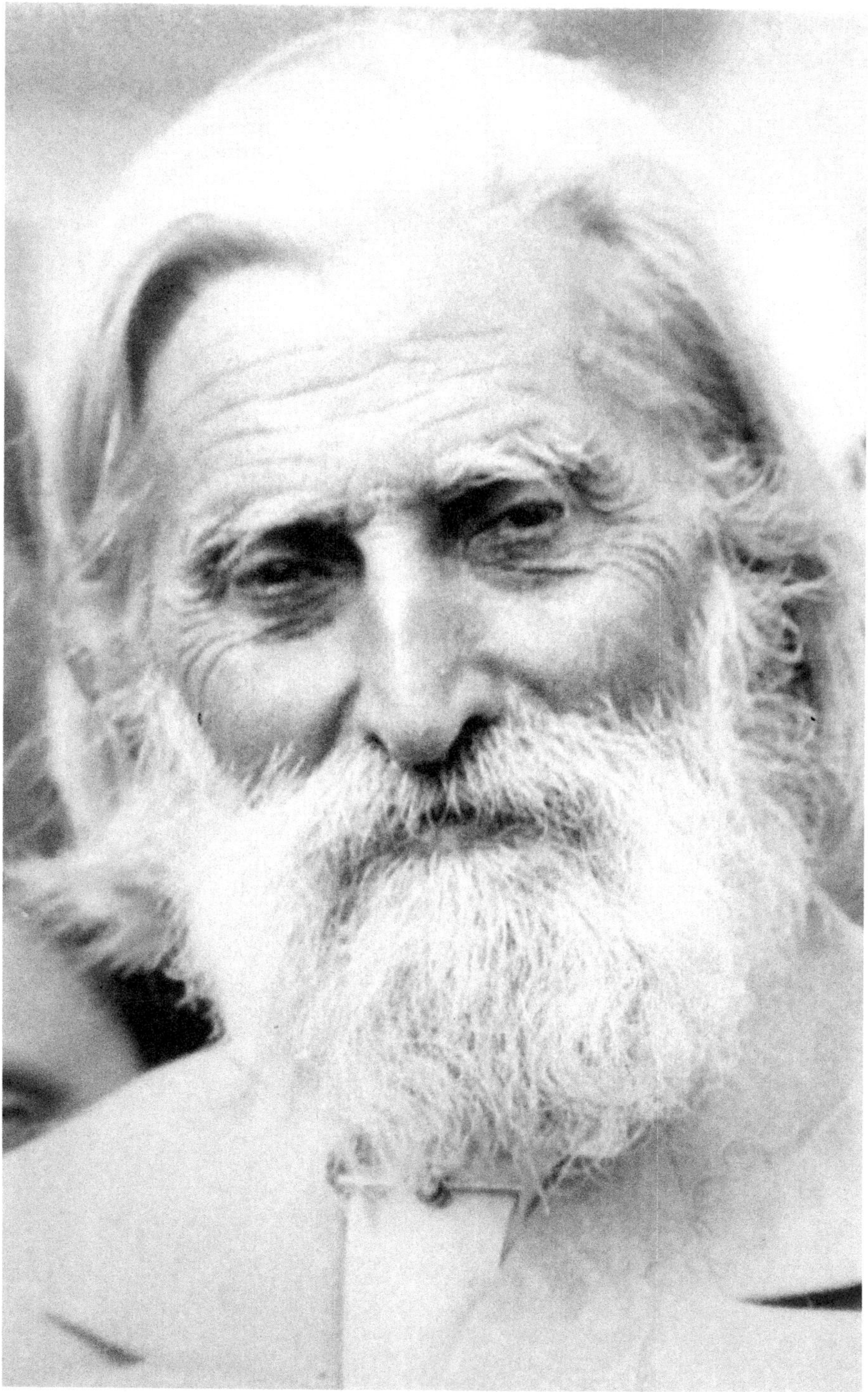

FOREWORD

The book is comprised of thoughts that I have collected from lectures given by the master Beinsa Douno/Peter Deunov. With a few exceptions, the thoughts are laid out in the order that I have read and selected from the lectures. They may look like jumping from one type of idea to another, but that's how they were often given by the master in the lectures. In my opinion, in short, this teaching in the book is a compass and a road map to the Kingdom of God. Of course not everything is said in the book, but the most important Divine principles are. Our job is to do the walk, i.e., to apply them. This teaching gives knowledge of how to ennoble yourself, how to become a good, loving, and righteous person; it gives knowledge about Divine Love, Wisdom, and Truth. The goal of the master is to make us think and love. I have tried my best to translate the meaning and the "spirit" of the Divine ideas that the master Beinsa Douno gave. I have used the word "man" to refer to both men and women, as it is used in the Bible, "God created man, both male and female," to keep the book in accordance with spirituality. In his lectures the master oftentimes used symbols and examples to describe certain ideas so that they can become easier to understand. He was also taking into account the culture and the level of development of the people (the Bulgarians) whom he was teaching at that specific time – from the beginning of the twentieth century up to the end of 1944 when he passed away. But the fundamentals of the Divine ideas are the same and they apply equally for each and every person, nation, and culture; and some of those fundamental Divine ideas that I collected are the ones that I am sharing with you. This is a teaching of Love, Wisdom, Truth, Justice/Righteousness, and Virtue.

This is a teaching fundamentally based on Christianity, explained and developed in more details. In order to get the most of the thoughts and the ideas, you have to analyze each thought well enough. Do not rush; try them out, thus you will discover the riches in them. By doing this you will slowly transform your way of thinking and character for the better. It is very important to start small. Better read and understand deeply one idea a day; but learn it very well. Learning one idea at a time is better than a dozen and forgetting about them soon thereafter. I have taken from each lecture anywhere from one to a few thoughts. The master was giving usually one lecture a week for the general class. So even if you completely absorb the meaning of a few ideas a weak, you will be doing just as well as his best followers at that time. Reasoning over the ideas and putting them into practice is what will give you the most fruits. You might not be able to understand the meaning of every thought right away, but that should not discourage you because some of them require more knowledge and will take you more time to comprehend. But once you understand them you will be glad you put the efforts to find the treasure hidden in them. Sometimes the students asked the master, "What we have learned so far?" (Maybe they were disappointed that they didn't get the knowledge of how to make from one thousand loaves of bread from one, or how to perform miracles.) To that the master replied, "You have learned the 9 signs, but the last one you will get when you deny yourself from private property." The invisible world does not reveal its secrets just to anyone, but only to those who are ready. Some people today may ask if the master Beinsa Douno performed miracles to verify that he was a master. The answer is, yes he made many miracles, but only when he considered it right.

One can find that the knowledge Beinsa Douno gives in the lectures sometimes looks like we already know it, or looks very simple, but in my opinion, right there we often miss getting the most out of it because we do not apply it in our daily lives, and do not make the ideas part of our character or part of our principles. One very useful advice from the master - "Go out and read the best books in the world."

If you like this book you may want to check the books "The Might of Love", and "Prayers and Spiritual Formulas" as
well. All three are available for free (digital format). To get a free copy of the e-books send an email to: mainpem@gmail.com.
You are welcome to share them with everyone who might be interested.
Enjoy your reading.

Peace, Love, and Light.
Darin Stoytchev

When Love reigns, disturbance does not come. When Wisdom rules, order does not get broken. When Truth beams, fruit blossoms.

Love is a way through which life comes. Wisdom is a way through which light and reason come. Truth is a way through which freedom is acquired.

When man does not accept Love, he loses his life. When man denies Reason, he loses his light and falls into darkness and into a no-way-out situation. When he abandons Truth, he loses his freedom. Then slavery comes.

The one who gives always gains more than the one who takes.

God forgives then only when people do not steal or lie.

The world will improve when you improve yourself.

The new culture requires of man to love God. Where will he find God? In everyone!

Love looks like the smallest power, but it is the greatest one! It begins with the weak things, but ends up with the greatest. If you acquire Love, you acquire the help of thousands and billions of souls.

Happiness lies in this: Be pleased with the little you have; be pleased with the life you have. It is recommended to have something little with no worries rather than something big and have worries with it.

Every thought, no matter how elementary it is, that brings peace in man's heart is preferred over all those "great" thoughts that bring anxiety.

The man in whom never arises the desire to hurt himself or others only he possesses Divine consciousness.

Without Love in the world, the new will not be able to come. Now I want from you, if it is possible, to apply the smallest Love. To apply the smallest Love rests in this: not to disturb the Lord in you.

There is nothing more positive for all of you than to learn right speech. In right speech, I understand that there should not be hidden in you any negative thoughts or wishes, not even a single one. Also, you should be pleased with every act of yours. In addition, you should be pleased with every feeling that comes in you. That is the right life.

A man with patience is that one who hears out everyone. A good man is the one who does not get indignant from evil.

The good is God in the world.

You need to aspire every day, to perceive every day one good thought, one good feeling, and to do one good deed.

If you don't have an excellent mind and an excellent heart, you will not be able to nurture a positive thought or a positive feeling in yourself.

What is a lie? The smallest mistake in the world that leads to great dangers. Which people lie? The weak and the unreasonable people lie, not the strong and reasonable. The one who lies is a weak man.

When you love somebody, you are ready to do anything for him. You have to give him freedom, but not blackmail him. You need to be so delicate and careful with his mind, heart, and soul with the person you love, that within him there should not remain a thought that you want to use him, but instead that you want to sacrifice yourself for him. If he is left with the thought that you want to use him, he is done with you.

We cannot learn that art of loving each other without serving. Serving is needed, not imposed, but done voluntarily.

Love that begins with joy is human Love; Love that begins with great suffering is Divine.

Contemporary people know almost nothing about Love. It is in store for you from now on to study the law of Love.

In order to acquire Love, you need humility. When humility comes, knowledge will come, and Love will follow.

Remove from yourself the thought of superiority over others. Know that every man, every soul, has the opportunity to ennoble and elevate him-, itself.

The one who serves God is in the condition to accept the Love of God. God will teach you how to love. Serve, so you can strengthen your Love. To serve God means to let the Divine pass through you without any hindrances.

The first thing that Love requires is this: When you meet someone, find at least one lofty trait in his character for which you can love him.

Think good for others! When a man thinks good for others, he thinks good for himself.

The echo of every thought of yours will come back to you. You will hear it one day. If you keep in your mind the bad energy about somebody, it will make an imprint in your brain and you will resemble that man.

To keep people's good traits in your mind and not criticize anyone are a sure method for developing Love.

Thank God for that which He gave you, for the opportunities you have, and for everything else. In that way, you will acquire God's Love.

That which you love in man is the inner, the invisible thing. That thing is the real thing.

In order to love somebody, there must be some reason for the Love. There must be something in him that you can love.

It is good to love somebody. To love somebody means to discover some virtue in him that has been hidden in him for eternity, to discover the Truth that lives in him, the Wisdom that lives in him, and the Love that lives in him.

You can love somebody for his gifts, knowledge, and so on. But that is not Love of the real man. Divine Love is Love toward the man himself.

You cannot know a man until you come to love him.

The first sign of a man manifesting Love is his inner peace. At the same time, he also has an aspiration toward the limitless, toward the lofty.

To the one who loves a lot, a lot is given.
To the one who loves a little, a little is given.
The one who loves a lot knows a lot.
The one who loves a little knows a little.
To love all, this is for the advanced souls.

Everyone's task is to manage to get into the inner, the mystical side of Love.

Those who commit crimes do not have a comprehension of Love. As soon as you come to know Love, crime and sin will cease. Until you come to know it, you will be making mistakes. The one who loves cannot commit any crimes. **Why in Love can crime not exist? Because God is present there!**

The one who loves no one can tempt him.

A man of Divine Love, this is the nicest and the most beautiful thing we can meet.

Love begins with the awakening of the conscience.

Love and don't be afraid. It is less dangerous to love than not to.
I love, but I suffer, I have fear. If you have fear, you have no Love. Love does not tolerate any fear.

Give a little, but from your heart.

Apply Love, and your life will be set right. Which love? The one you are ready for.

It is good to be loved, but by the righteous, not by the sinners. If you are loved by the sinners, that means they will give you their weakness, from which you will not be able to get rid of for years. When a sinner loves you, through his Love he can do you a great deal of harm. It is preferred the sinners not to love you than to have their Love.

Love people without connecting yourself with their weaknesses.

As a reality, Love expresses itself through these four things: It brings light in the mind, warmth in the heart, nobleness in the soul, and strength in the spirit. Without Love, no reasonable deed can happen. Without Love, no one can elevate himself.

The one who loves leaves in all beings something valuable.

If you run the strong vibrations of Divine Love, the ones that the cherubs and the seraphim have through a man, he will be transformed to light, but won't understand those things.

With Love are met the greatest contradictions.

When the weak stands in the way of Love, it bypasses him so that it does not run over him.

When you love somebody, you are a conductor, a witness of the Love that God sends through you. That is how a man should think.

Whoever wants to enter a world higher than this one, he should enter the world of Love.
This that lives and does not die is Love. This that lives and dies is from the temporarily things.

There is no greater teaching than Love.

You have had ordinary Love, but that one Love that frees man you have not tried yet.

Love between people is not manifested in a single life alone.

Love comes out of God and returns back to God again.

It is better Love be inside of you than outside of you.

What is Love? A power that does not allow hatred.

What has been built without Love always has been destroyed, for the foundation of things is Love, and without a foundation, nothing can be built.

When we say that we have to be strong, we understand that we have to be strong in Divine Love.

For a man to become strong in the world, he must first begin with Love. A man is strong as long as Love lives in his soul. The very moment Love leaves him, he becomes weak.

Why do you suffer? To acquire Love. What do you need Love for? To free yourself from suffering.

The one who loves you holy, when he departs for the invisible world, he is still around you. He thinks constantly of you. He does everything for you. After he dies, he can help you ten times more than while being physically alive.

Lovelessness gives birth to hatred, but Love to life.

What is material Love? A bottle that contains only a liter of water. How many people can be served with that water? Only five or six people.

The one who has real Love will give and will not ask you for anything in return. But the one who gives a thing and asks you for ten in return, he is manifesting human Love.

If people had Love, they would have put themselves in other people's place to help each other.

Everyone has a certain mission on Earth. No one has come in vain.

Where there is no Love, violence exists. Violence cannot be eliminated by using violence as a way to stop it.

There is a law in the world that manifests itself if acted with Love. The little things we do, the good, keep growing.

If you have Love, you will have everything. If you don't have it, you will lose everything.

No matter how unfavorable conditions you might have, if you apply Love, it will elevate and improve them. Firstly, this Love will change your mind, heart, and will, it will change the environment around you, the people around you will soften, and your life will become more decent.

Behind light sits Love. Behind power sits Love. Behind discontent, sin, again sits Love. The only power that directs and corrects everything in the world is Love. You say, "Is it possible for Love to sit behind sin?" Love sits behind sin, because in this case, it has not manifested itself, but waits for a propitious moment to do so. The one who does not know Love, he always commits sins, crimes. As soon as he comes to know it, any sin, any crime, will disappear.

One of the qualities of Love is consistency, invariability. He who really loves, he never changes. If people have changed their Love for you, know that they have never loved you.

Love even when they don't love you. Regardless of whether they love you or not, love. For whomever your Love may be directed, it must be hidden from people's eyes.

He who talks a lot about his Love, he will be put to a test, which he will hardly pass. The nicest Love is that one of which people do not know. Only you and God should know about it, but not other people. When you meet the one whom you love, you will feel in yourself an inspiration. A single look at him is enough for that.

Love has this quality: You elevate that one whom you love.

Have an absolute trust in that one whom you love and the one who loves you.

If you love somebody, never ask if he deserves your Love. He deserves it. Whomever you may love, he deserves your love, because you love the Divine soul in him. Never say, "I am sorry I loved him." With Love you have not lost anything. You and he have gained.

If you love somebody and he starts becoming good, your Love is Divine. If he does not become good, your Love is human. Divine Love makes man sound, healthy, strong, and good.

When you love somebody, simultaneously with acquiring his good qualities, you also acquire his bad ones. This happens with ordinary Love. When good people love the bad, they are doing them good. When a good man loves a bad man, the good man should not worry about the danger, the bad energies, he could receive. Because in the end, if his Love is strong and Divine, it will transform the bad energies.

The bad people, as they love the good, they are doing themselves a favor, because they become conductors of the good energies of the good people.

In the Divine world, when you give something from yourself, you acquire. Every good deed that you have made, it is you who will try out its fruits first.

A man who does not know how to study and how to serve cannot achieve anything. He will have ordinary results like everyone else.

Whatever a man thinks, whatever a man feels, and in whatever way he acts, this all will reflect on his body. A man with his thoughts, his feelings, and his deeds creates his own future.

All people are created to be good, but not all are good. All people are created to be rich, but not all are. All people are created to be in good health, but not all are healthy. The reason is in them themselves.

When you meet a good man, he gives, but takes nothing. When you meet a righteous man, you take something from him. You say, "I wish I were like him." To be like him means to constantly give. You need to think like him, not to be taking. You need to work; man has to constantly work on himself.

Love is that inner process that sets thoughts in their places, sets feelings in their places, and sets man's health in its place.

When you love somebody, you begin to constantly teach him not to do this, not to do that. But Love does not like to be given any advice. Whomever you love, do not give him advice. If you love someone and he makes a mistake, close your eyes and do not pay attention to his mistakes. When you come to Love, do not look for any mistakes. All the mishaps come out of this, that we correct the love at home. (My personal explanation on this is: When people start correcting one another, then the arguments come, and then somebody may feel offended for some reason.)

Outside of Love, it is commonplace to correct. But with Love, you cannot. With Love, if you quit making corrections, things will go better.

Love is the most dynamic thing. When it comes, it cleanses all sediments that the man has.

The light in the mind is the Love; the warmth in the heart is the Love; the strength in the body is the Love.

Now, when it is spoken about life, life is important to us so much, as much it can give us something good. We are interested in this thought as much it can uplift and elevate our mind. We are interested in Love as much as it can elevate our heart.

Love is the greatest harmony that exists in the world. When you enter Love, you will not know what suffering means.

If I love, I am the one who benefits from that. The one who accepts my Love, he benefits from it too. If I do not love, I harm myself. If the one I love does not accept my Love, he harms himself. This law has no exceptions.

When will the world be set right? When Love becomes the master, when compassion becomes the master, when greed the servant, and fear the servant, then the world will be set right.

Cosmic Love is Love from the center toward the fringes. The world's Love is Love from the fringes toward the center.

What is "bad"? "Bad" is a material world whose laws you do not know. The bad rests in the double standards one uses in his relations with others. If you use one standard only, you are a good man. If you use double standards, you are a bad man.

If somebody wants to be good to obtain recognition from others that he is a good man, he is walking on the wrong path. Wondering whether people think you are good or bad is wrongful thinking. I have to be good because good is the foundation of life. I have to be good for myself. If I am good, I am a conductor of the Divine. If I am not good, I am not a conductor of the Divine. If a man does not have the good as a foundation, he cannot expect any achievements in the future. And whatever he has built will collapse.

If you want your situation to improve, have the nicest thoughts. Think well in order to have always light in your mind. Feel well in order to have always warmth in your heart and your heart to beat evenly.

Everything and whatever may happen to you in the world, when you enter the Divine world will be for your good.

When it comes to God, have a holy thought. Have an opinion that whatever the Lord does is for good. Let us be pleased with that, what He gives us.

As soon as man stops to love, he gets sick. The distorted Love brings all the mishap and misunderstanding in the world.

If you love your father and your mother, your life will be extended. If you do not love your father, your mother, your brother, your life will be shortened. This law has been ascertained from time immemorial.

Always make a connection with all good people. Make a connection with smart people. Make a connection with fair people. You have to constantly make a connection with good people, with smart and fair people, so that there can be an exchange between you. If you do not make a connection with the Good, you cannot become good. If you do not make a connection with fairness, you cannot become fair. If you do not make a connection with smart people, you cannot become smart.

Make a connection with every man through whom God is manifested.

Love is unchangeable. It gives and leaves. Love does not stay. It leaves you something and departs. It will not ask you: "Are you content?" If you are content, you are content, but if you are not, it won't start convincing you. There is not such a thing in Divine Love as "convincing." It leaves you exactly that what you need. If you use it, good, if not, the next time it will leave you another good. It comes and leaves us the third and forth good, and in the end we are still not happy, because that good that God has given us, we have not put to use.

Money is not the most important thing in life. It is just a tool. The most important thing in life is to have light. The second most important thing is warmth, and the third most important is strength.

Everything in the world that happens without Love is a crime. Everything in the world that happens with Love is a Divine blessing.

Where Love does not participate, where Wisdom and Truth do not take part, those actions are a crime. But where Love, Wisdom, and Truth take part, it is God's blessing.

No man is free if he is not penetrated by God's Love, God's Wisdom, and God's Truth.

Truth sits in this: in the worst to see the nice, the good.

Patient can be the strong man only. The weak man cannot be patient. God is patient.

Firstly, we need to become strong. Naturally, to become strong in heart and strong in mind, a long time of work is required.

It is easier to correct the bad in you than in others.

Money is a spoiled woman; it gives a smile to everyone.

Now you want to please God. If you do not rectify those mistakes that only you see, you cannot please Him.

The strong man is that one who knows how to rectify the invisible mistakes he makes. Everyone who rectifies his mistakes receives reward. When they get rectified, he won't be judged for them.

Contemporary people have learned to steal. Because they have no Love, they have no faith in God. God created all good things on Earth for people. Ask Him, and He will give to you. Whatever you want, there is no need to steal.

True comprehension of life lies in Love of God. Love of God is the beginning of things. Love of your neighbor is the solution of things.

People have put aside the Love of God and their neighbor, but have put the Love of themselves in the first place. As a consequence, there is a division among people.

People should know that happiness does not lie outside man. Man can acquire happiness only when he acquires the Spirit in himself.

When people ask themselves how could they rectify or improve their lives, I say people's lives can be improved when Love reigns in their hearts, when Wisdom reigns in their minds, and when Truth reigns in their spirit.

The Lord is not some outer object that needs to be proven. He is not in time and space; He is outside of time and space.

Love is invisible, but is real. When Love enters somebody, if he happens to be rude, cruel, or ferocious, he right away transforms into softness, is ready to do any favors, make any sacrifices.

There is no scarier poison in the world than a lie. It is the scariest poison because it is the hardest to get rid of. Nothing is more dangerous in man's life than a lie.

All people's mishaps sit in the untruthful things. When a man puts a lie as a foundation in his life, all mishaps will certainly meet him.

How can a man find out which deed is Divine? When he thinks not for himself, but for others, that deed is Divine. But when a man thinks for himself only, he always commits a crime.

All crimes in the world are due to those conditions in which man thinks for himself alone.

Faith is only a way to God. But to know just this way does not benefit you anything.

Who is a righteous man? A righteous man is that one who is connected with Love, with the eternal beginning. A righteous man is that one who is led by Love's law. When man bears Love in himself, he is so rich that he does not need anything from anybody.

The one who wants to take only is the one who commits crime. This fact has been verified already.

People cannot have any Love either for themselves or for their neighbors unless they fall in love with God.

All mishaps in the world emerge from not applying the great law—the Love of God—the way we should.

Love is the bearer of true freedom.

With Love, there is a choice, but in the old philosophy, there are not any choices.

Love is this without which no life can exist. Wisdom is this without which no movement can exist. Truth is this without which no border can exist.

The only thing in the world that does not evolve and remains unchangeable, and absolute, is God.

You have somebody, a friend of yours, whom you love. The higher your views of him are, the better for you, because he will be as ready to do you favors as you will be for him. The lower your views of him are the less is his ability to sacrifice himself for you.

You can never elevate a man unless you go down to his level. You need to go down to him to pick up his defects, his sins and crimes. You have to come down to his situation where he is and from there, as a smart soul, to solve his issues. If you do not do so, you cannot help him.

Love is the power that models things. Why should we love? You need to love, because through loving, you model yourself. If you do not love, you will remain a mediocre man, and you will not progress, for progress is possible only with Love.

Good comes from God, remember Him.

Freedom excludes any violence, any evil, any lie.

If you don't love, if you envy, you are weak people, and you belong to a world from which you will never free yourself unless you start loving.

There are three qualities in the strong man: He is a man of overabundant Love, overabundant life, overabundant knowledge and Wisdom, and overabundant freedom and Truth. Consequently, the strength of a man is a result of this that he has in himself.

How can a man get rid of his hatred? When he transforms it into Love. How can he get rid of his fear? When he transforms it into belief. How can you transform in you that one power of destruction? When you transform it into compassion.

In Heaven, that well-organized world, in the world of Love, go only those people who do the will of God. The rich who do the will of God go to Heaven, and the poor who do the will of God go to Heaven. But the poor and the rich who do not do the will of God do not go to Heaven.

The one who is a Love candidate wants to enter the Divine world. The one who wants good is a candidate for the spiritual world, and the one who wants health is a candidate for the physical world. Consequently, first want health, then good, and at last Love, so that it can support the health and good in you.

Christ says, "If you love me, you will keep my commandments, my law." Which law is that? The law of happiness. Man's happiness sits in one thing, to love. If he loves everyone, that means he is happy. If he loves just one, he is unhappy. When man loves just one, he is manifesting human Love, not Divine Love.

When you perform good actions in the world, think about Love. Let it be the stimulus in your life.

Which belief is the most right one? For me, the most right belief is that one that resurrects man, by enlightening one's mind, ennobling one's heart, improving life, and bringing peace, joy, and merriment among all people. That is the right belief.

Faith is a way for achievement. The best things in the world in all fields have happened through faith.

This that you wish people comes back to you. Now until New Years Eve, when you meet your friends, wish them the best, without talking many superfluous words.

Love always has a feeling, a desire to give a favor, to help. Love does not discriminate between one and another being.

When you love one, but not the other, and when you see a difference between one and another man, you have not understood the will of God. It is hard to love man.

There are certain thoughts in you that like plants you have to grow with care. There are certain thoughts in the mental world that are like plants and we must sow them in our minds. Also, there are certain feelings that are like plants and that we have to sow in our hearts.

If you cannot plant a thought in your mind, and a feeling in your heart, and care for them as you would like fruit trees, you will never educate yourself. Every thought and every feeling that you grow in yourself must produce a fruit. You have some thoughts and feelings in you that produce no fruit; those are fruitless trees.

He who has comradeship with Love and Wisdom, he always remains unbeatable. Because he has in himself the greatest warmth and light, no one can do him any mischief. Do you know what kind of warmth that is? From that warmth even the hairs of the devil stand on end.

Make friendship with Love to see how all of your enemies will run away. All enemies, but his friends, disappear before the man of Love.

Put yourself to work for your heart, for your mind, for your will, so that when you meet Christ, He will tell you: "Be brave, go ahead, that is the way!"

To love somebody means in a given situation to do for him the same sacrifice as you would do for yourself, without hesitation, without having a conflict of two morals inside yourself.

Fear is an unreasonable condition. When man does not understand the laws, he gets scared.

Man will enter the kingdom of God with his little good deeds that no one has seen. With these little good deeds as your ornaments, your virtues, you will enter the kingdom of God.

Now as I say that, I don't want by any means to stimulate greed in you or for you to do good actions for the sake of being good. No, the singer should sing to bring merriment to people, nothing more! Get up and sing!

When you talk about Love, Wisdom, Truth, and virtue, your mouth should always be pure. If one's mouth is not pure, he may say bad things. It will be nice for you to always keep your mouth pure. That means to never allow unclean vibrations to come out of your mouth. Imagine what it would mean to tell somebody that you hate him, that you don't want to see him, that you don't trust him, and so on. Do not make your tongue dirty with the remains of the past generation! Tell yourself: "I will live; I will study to acquire God's strengths. I will love all people on Earth, I will do what God wants me to do, I will perform good actions, and so on."

If we go by the law of harmony of the great Divine world, there will be good and people will always be attracted to us around us.

For every bad thought that has passed through your mind, you bare no responsibility for it. Strive to replace it with a good one, but do not strive to kick it out. If some bad feeling has come in your heart, do not fight with it, but put in its place a good one. If a feeling of strictness has come in your heart, replace it with a feeling of compassion. If a feeling of selfishness has come in your heart, put in its place a feeling of humanity.

Life without Love is a life of worries. But life with Love is a life of calmness, work, labor, health, strength, freedom, space, and movement.

A smart man is one who does not bring on himself unneeded suffering. Every man who brings on himself unneeded suffering does not possess a strong intellect. His intellect is a mediocre one.

There is one chosen nation in the world, but this nation is neither the English, nor the Jewish, nor any other nation. This nation is the whole of humanity as one unit. This nation chosen by God is comprised of all beings, of all people who think, because man is distinguished namely by his thought. That is how I define man.

In the meantime, I say the man who rectifies his mistakes, he is a man. He who does not rectify his mistakes, he is an animal. You can think whatever you like; that is how I understand it. An animal is distinguished by this, that it cannot rectify its mistakes. The wolf will remain a wolf for thousands upon thousand of years. Boil it … bake it …, a wolf it will remain. Even if it gets four bachelor degrees, a wolf it will remain.

Truth cannot be old or young. It cannot grow old, nor rejuvenate itself. Truth is that beginning that renders the eternal process of development, that beginning that brings meaning to life. The whole world sits in Truth; behind Truth, there is no other meaning.

The only thing that brings meaning to the life of people is Truth. And when we have joy and merriment, it is the Truth that has caused that joy.

When a man achieves something in the world, he is in the world of Truth. All human achievements are due to the Truth.

If a man loves Truth, it always will help him. The man who lives and moves in Truth will be helped by it; Truth is reasonable.

Believe that in everything in the world, in the good and in evil, is God! That is by principle. If you understand God, He is manifesting Himself as good in you. If you don't understand Him, He is manifesting Himself as evil in you. When you repent, He stops tormenting you.

Everything is inside God. Evil is created by us, because we want to influence the Lord, to make Him think like us. But that's impossible.

That Love that connects people as one and puts them in a situation to understand each other and to work together, that is Divine Love. Love in which each and everyone is ready to make for the other such sacrifices as he is ready to do for himself, this is true Love.

I often talk about Love, but this Love is not the one people think of as Love. I think happy life flows out of Love, but Love does not live in life; it is outside of life. Love is not in reasonable life; it manifests itself *through* reasonable life, but it is outside reasonable life. Love is a great power in the world. When it comes, it gives only, and leaves.

Right thought is having in mind the needs of your neighbor as your own.

Sacrifice is a voluntarily act, which has a relationship to the law of Love, not to the law of violence.

Never marry without Love. Never give birth to children without Love. If you have no Love, do not marry. Marriage is a Divine institution ... a Divine service.

Love allows man to marry once only. If he marries a few times, that is the work of a human, work outside of Love.

God requires the least from man. He says, "Love your enemy"—the first stage of Love.

"Love your neighbor like yourself"—the second stage of Love.

"Love God with all your might, with all your heart, with all your soul, with all your strength"—the third stage of Love.

Love begins with ordinary Love, toward your neighbor.

Love includes everything in itself. In it are knowledge, power, riches, reason, and good. Knowing this, do not seek for these things outside yourself.

He who has tried to find out who loves him and how has already lost Love. The beauty of life sits in this, to love.

This that gives power in man is the Truth in him, the good in him. Truth and good are qualities of the Divine in man. Without Truth and good, there are no relations.

Without Truth and good, no home … no society exists.

What is required from us? The rich to help the poor. Give to others as you want to be given to.

To love somebody means to free him. As you love, you free yourself and the surroundings. If you love somebody, but you don't give him freedom, you are not in the way of light. You are not manifesting God's love.

Love supports life. Wisdom supports light and knowledge. Truth supports freedom.

The basic element of life is Love. Light, knowledge, and freedom are conditions for Love's manifestation. They represent the outer side of life.

The easiest is the road of Love. The road of Wisdom requires great knowledge, and the possibilities for it are less.

Love must flow in constantly to the human soul. It is life's food. Knowing this, every feeling and deed must be filled with Love. Remember, God stands behind and watches every word and thought of ours.

Until people become equalized, they cannot be brothers and sisters. That means everyone must consider the rights of the other, as he considers his own. Love understands the inner consideration of all holy rights of the soul.

Without Love of God, happiness does not exist. Man's happiness is in freedom, his unhappiness in slavery. Man's happiness is in Love, unhappiness in hatred. Man's happiness is in knowledge and light, unhappiness in ignorance and darkness.

First, love God, do His will. Then love yourself. From the love of God, you will learn how to love your neighbor and yourself. Thus, you will learn how to help and whom to help.

I wish you to be free of the worries of the world so that you can voluntarily do the will of God.

In God's love is man's good.

Man cannot live in the world for himself alone.

Reason guides us to live rightly, in the light.

Do not feel sorry for anything, but constantly make an effort of your own. No matter how microscopic that effort is, do not get discouraged. You can have thousands of slips a day, but that should not deter you.

Under the word God, I understand the only being who never changes. He is a being who has no limit; He is infinite. God is a being who disposes with all things, and does things the way He finds is good. Consequently, behind Him there is no other being. For Him there is no law. He Himself is law. Be always in alignment with Him, and you will see how your life will change. It will be set right. If people would have understood this great law, their lives would have changed in a moment.

Love sits before everything else, higher than any comprehension. Love precedes reason. Reason is the result of Love. When it is said that God is Love, it should be known that Love is that which arranges all works in the world.

To love somebody means to give him the best food to eat, the cleanest water to drink, the freshest air to breathe, the best books to read, and lastly to put him in the nicest place.

Happiness is something great. When it comes to happiness, man should be very smart. In order for man to be happy, he must be something more than a saint. Even the saint cannot be completely happy. There is happiness in one condition only. Happiness is a result of Divine Love. He who lives in this Love can only be happy.

If the rich want to keep their riches, they must be generous, and pure. Who can be pure? Only the honest and just man can be pure. That is how I interpret purity. I think purity is a symbol, an emblem of fairness and honesty.

A generous man is a man of Love. You cannot be generous if Love has not permeated your soul. If you are rich and you want to keep your riches, you must love all people around you and be honest and fair. Then all people around you will cooperate with you and thus you will create a family.

For his happiness, man must be diligent, man must be generous, and man must be pure.

Man can never be happy if he has not gone through the school of poverty and the school of riches. In that situation only can a man be happy. Consequently, poverty and riches are two schools for you to enter in life that bring happiness.

Love is proved only by trial.

Man's wealth depends on his mind. A man who possesses neither a wealthy mind nor a wealthy heart can never be wealthy.

Only the Divine in you, which gives you an impulse, should you rely on. The other things in you are also nice, but the Divine is the seed, the Divine is the power, the Divine is happiness in man's life. Upon it rests the health and happiness of a man's life, from one end to the other.

You cannot understand man if you do not love him. In addition, in this love, you should have no desire to restrict him.

One can live in trust with a reasonable man, but with a foolish man one cannot live in trust.

With Love everyone can be satisfied according to the level that he has. Do not want to be satisfied like other people are.

If you want to be happy and also want to be paid for your happiness, this is impossible. (For example, you cannot serve God and ask to be paid for it. The work for God is done for free, without financial remuneration.)

All crime is due to impure thoughts and wishes, which leaves in people certain impurities and surpluses.

God is a Consciousness in which all other consciousnesses reside. He strives to regulate all those consciousnesses in Himself.

Even in the most unfavorable conditions in life, you need to learn not to lose courage.

If you love God, you need to tell yourself, "Everything that I am going through is for the good," and the formula for solving issues, "This that I cannot solve God will solve." If you say this, you will see that the solution will come within twenty-four hours at the most, because it is not you who solves the issues in the world, but God.

This that satisfies the soul is Love. This that satisfies the spirit is Wisdom. This that gives meaning to everything is Truth.

Life without virtues is a garden without flowers, is trees without fruit. Do not seek what you do not need.

Love is extremely generous and extremely demanding.

If we do not put heart into serving God, we will achieve nothing.

Everyone who has tried to fight evil has always paid with his life. God, who understands the law, only He has the power to fight and defeat evil.

Between you and evil, put the God of Love.
If you always think about the bad traits in man, you boost the bad in him. If you think about his good traits, you boost the good in him.

The first crime in the world is to vilify a man. All crime is due to the impure thoughts and wishes that leave in people certain impurities and surpluses.

Strong people are those who transmit Love, weak people those who only accept love.

Only with Love are things real.

If you love somebody, you can bare all of his suffering. If you don't love him, you cannot bare even the lightest.

Whatever may happen to you, God is testing you.

How should life be comprehended? Consider that man's soul has emerged from God. The way you respect God is the same way you must respect the soul, because of God, who is in the soul.

There are three rules you need to keep in mind in order to free yourself from all your delusions:
- The first rule: Love is a way in life. If you want to free yourself from all delusions, you need to be in the consciousness of Love. Embracing Love, you will avoid the greatest mishaps.
- The second rule: The light of Wisdom is a way to knowledge. Consequently, if you do not

have this way, this light, you cannot acquire knowledge. If you do not have the light of Wisdom, you will not know how to arrange your life, and you will always find yourself in contradiction with the self.
- The third rule: Truth is a way to freedom. Consequently, if you are not in this way of Truth, you cannot be free.

These are maxims, formulas, for living.

When man does things according to God, he has in his disposition all the good people in the world. When man serves God wherever he goes, all doors are open for him.

If a man does not walk on the path of Wisdom, he cannot have light and knowledge. If a man does not walk on the path of Truth, he cannot have freedom.

Three rules for living:
- Make Love be a way in your life.
- Have Wisdom be a way for knowledge and light.
- Let Truth be a way for your freedom.

Apply this as a foundation, and you will avoid unneeded suffering and acquire everything you wish.

The scariest thing, from which man should be afraid, is the smallest lie. Never try to lie to yourself. When you come to the lie, tell yourself, this is a lie. The honest and noble man is the one who does not allow a lie. He can sin in different ways and all his sins can be forgiven. The only sin that nature does not forgive is a lie. The first people were kicked out of paradise not on account of their sin, but because of their lie.

The beauty of life for you sits in this—to love.

When a man achieves something in the world, he is in the world of Truth. All human achievements are due to the Truth.

If a man loves Truth, it will always help him. The man who lives and moves in Truth will always be helped; Truth is reasonable.

Believe that everything in the world, in the good and in evil, is God!

When two people love each other, the first thing that is required from them is to have mutual exchange. In this sits the meaning of life. Do not want to be loved only. Life sits in this—to love and to be loved.

Competition is a human process, not a Divine one.

A true brother for you is that one who is one with you in spirit, in soul, in mind, and in heart. True sisters or friends for you are only those who are one with you in mind, in heart, in spirit, and in soul. And they should share your fate in all conditions.

Until man comes to the situation to put his trust in Love, he is not on the right path.

What is Truth? This that in a given situation excludes from man all delusions, all evil deeds, all injustices, all evil, everything bad, but includes in it everything good, everything lofty, this is the Truth. This that in a given case brings in man life, meaning, and nobleness, this is the Truth. This that can take me from one condition and bring me into another one, this is the Truth; this that always has elevated me, and in the future will, this is the Truth. Truth has practical meaning in its application. Yet however I determine Truth, I am still not able to define it.

Law: No one can love you if you have not given him something from yourself. Children love their mother, because she has given them something from herself. We all love God, because He has given us a lot of things from Himself. We must love God, because everything we have He has given to us.

You must believe in God, in Love, because from the faith you have, from this Love, depends not only your happiness, but that of your wife, your children, and your family.

When it comes to Love, be ready for any sacrifices for it; then only will it be able to stand up for you.

Faith in the world: That faith, the love of God, when we make a connection with all people to live well, to love each other, to help each other, this faith is the faith in the world! It is without regard to nations, whichever they may be, Bulgarians or English, but these nations to mutually help each other.

We are loved not because of us alone; we are loved for that which resides in us, for the Divine.

Without the Divine in the world, no Love could exist, no happiness could exist; man's heart would not be able to progress.

Young is he who is ready to give favors to all. Young is that one who can bear any sufferings, who can bear all inconveniences. Young is that one who studies, who loves, who does not lie, who has no fear. Young is he who works and pays all his dues on time. Young is he who is set all right; whoever is not set all right is in old age.

Write down these sentences:
    1 Truth brings freedom to the reasonable.
    2 Love brings life to the good.

Love, which brings in warmth, gives all the materials with which you can work, Wisdom, the methods and the powers with which the mind can work, and Truth and space and broadness, the outer conditions with which you can accomplish everything you want. A man who possesses these three principles, Love, Wisdom, and Truth, can always succeed.

One becomes strong when he puts his fear at work.

In any given moment, you should know two things: whether you are doing your will or the will of God. If you are ready to serve God, He will change your life.

A fool is everyone who errs and does not rectify his mistakes. The fool always seeks the easy things; he cannot make the connection between the reasons and the consequences.

Do not secure yourself, because security is already a restriction. Do not secure a man, for the one who gets secured loses faith in himself.

Law in Love: When you love somebody and he takes some energy from you, it will soon get compensated.

Love's goal is freedom for the human soul.

Even in the worst things, see God hidden behind. The philosophy lies in this, in the greatest contradictions to see God. If you see in the disease God, you have already recovered your health.

Law: For as long man worries, his things won't be set right, and if he is sick, he will not be able to get cured. So, firstly, stop worrying and put behind the discontent, then your fate will set right easier.

You cannot have right thoughts until you have Love. You cannot think rightly for a man if you do not love him. Do not put off your work for tomorrow, for tomorrow has its own work, and you won't be able to finish two works successfully.

Love should be directed toward everything. Under "everything" is understood the whole, God, and everything that He has created.

What does a man need to succeed? He needs three things: the good or the virtue as a foundation, fairness with which he will be building, and reason to know how to approach others.

If you do not think right, you are not free. If you do not feel right, you are not free. If you do not do what is right, you are not free.

If somebody asserts that he loves you, but he puts a halter on you, this is not love.

Only with Love is there equality; for people to be equal, they have to love one another. A man who loves cannot commit a crime.

Love is a healthful condition of the soul.

This that gives opportunity for the human soul to develop, to grow, is the Divine, is Love.

How can one serve God? When he works among the people. When a man works upon himself, that is a preparation for serving God, and it can be accepted as doing God's work.

Man should not say, "I will serve God," but just do it, every day.

The formula; say it three times quietly: In God's limitless Love, there are joy and gaiety for all souls.

The most efficient method for curing is Love. When you become the conduit of God's Love, the disease momentarily disappears. Boost your love and the disease will go away. If you have Love, you will have health.

The sick man should never allow any negative thoughts in his mind.

Tell sick people who are asking for help to do the will of God.

When one is sick, he can say, "In the name of God's Love, in the name of God's Wisdom, in the name of God's Truth, I am commanding you to leave. I live with Love. Love excludes any disease. My body is a temple of God; therefore, it should have no disease."

Health in the world emerges from Love. If you love, you are healthy. If you do not love, you are sick. All diseases in the world come out of the lack of love.

Love and you will be rich and happy and the world will open itself to you.

Good and evil does not exist in Heaven. Good and evil are for Earth. You think that if you become good you will go to Heaven. Good is a dress for Earth, not for Heaven. To go to Heaven, you need to go with the dress of Love.

Live like a human, think like an angel, and love like God loves. That is a science.

Strong is that one whom nobody can rob from this which he has.

The good life is a result of something. You cannot live well if you have not thought well, if you have not felt well. The good life is a result of thought. The good depends firstly on Love. The Good depends also on thought, and then as a result comes the good life.

How can we liquidate the past? There are three ways only: That can be done only through the law of Love, the law of thought, and the law of good—that is how karma gets liquidated.

Law: Love others like you love yourself. The most idealistic is to love God.

Law: With any help you can give others you are helping yourself.

If you are content with riches, but discontent when they are taken away from you, you have not understood Love. Be content in both cases and give thanks. Riches and titles can be given and taken away from you, but believe in Love that bears in itself all good things, and these good things will be given to you at the time when you are ready.

If you fall in love with health, you will become healthy. If you fall in love with the good, you will become good. Whatever you fall in love with that's what you will become.

Everything you do, do it with Love.

If you expect from people to make your character, your mind, and your heart good, you will never have them. You yourself can create for yourself a character, a mind, and a heart whatever you may want them to be.

Our sufferings emerge from this, that our love is not like Divine Love. We need to begin loving our neighbor like ourselves. Three things are needed: to love God with all your mind, soul, and strength. Love your neighbor like yourself. Then learn to love yourself. Unless you learn to love God the way you are supposed to, and your neighbor like yourself, you will not understand the world in which we live. When you love God, when you learn to love God, and your neighbor as yourself the way you should, then the true law will come to you: "Everything you ask will be given to you." It is said, "Seek first the kingdom of God and His justice, and everything else will be given to you." But these things are achievable only with Love. If you have in you this Divine Love, if you have love toward God, if you love yourself and your neighbor, then things are achievable.

A man without Love is a bird without wings, but a man with Love is a bird with wings, which descends and climes up freely.

Everyone who does not understand Love will burn out. But everyone who understands it will be blessed.

When in difficulty, how do you resolve the issues easier? With strength or with mind? With mind issues are resolved easier.

Keep this thought in mind: Love requires the greatest sacrifices. Everyone must make a sacrifice for God. Everyone should say for that one who has given everything, "For Him I am ready to make the greatest sacrifices." He should not talk much about this, because if he talks a lot, it loses power. There is no need to talk much about it.

Evil in the world cannot be kicked out with evil. If you kicked it out, it becomes stronger. Replace evil with good.

If you want to be strong, never allow a bad thought to enter your mind, a bad feeling to enter your heart, and a bad deed to enter your will. That is what is needed if you want to be strong.

Love, that brings life. Love, that brings light and knowledge. Love, that brings freedom for man's soul. That Love is Divine Love.

Remember, if you chase Love, that is not Love. There is no greater crime than that, to chase Love. There is no greater lie than two people wanting to out-lie each other in their Love.

To love somebody means to be blind to all his mistakes.

Love is that which makes you strong and powerful, which makes you immortal. Our goal is to become immortal. I say only Love will make you immortal.

In my view, you should have one fear only: losing Divine Love. I wish that you could have only one virtue in the world, to love God and your neighbor. That is enough. If you have that fear of losing Love and have that goodness to love God, then things are achievable for you.

Defeat evil with good, because through the good, you will find the meaning of life. Love is the only thing you should think about.

There is no equality outside of Love. Outside of Love is eternal inequality. Inside Love is eternal equality. Inside Love all conditions and all possibilities are achievable.

Man's life achievement is infinite Divine Love.

In Love there is no broken heart. In Love there is no unhappiness. In Love are all opportunities. When a man enters Love, in him immediately come joy, rejuvenation, and riches, everything comes, he can travel everywhere.

The one who has sacrificed everything for Love, he has won everything.

Whichever home, whichever mind, whichever heart, whichever body Love steps in, all things start to move forward. This is the condition of Divine Love.

The rays of Love are the connection among people.

Are you in trouble? Turn to Love for help—God is Love.

Blame and critique are steps to hatred, but help and good to Love.

What does it mean to live with good and noble thoughts and wishes? To have an understanding of a tree with good fruit.

Keep your mind and heart clean—speak the Truth. Truth, Wisdom, and Love are inseparable. Think for others as for people who love you and who think good for you.

Having a clear idea about God is like having a light in a tunnel. Loving Wisdom and Truth is loving God. Helping others is serving God, is helping yourself. There are two kinds of help: help for free and help for money. The first one comes from God, the second one from man.

You are what your real knowledge is in relation to Wisdom and Love. Being a good student rejoices God.

If you do good and get paid for it, your good does not count in Heaven. Do good without expectation to get anything in return to build a treasure in Heaven.

The song of Love is pleasure to the ears. Sing songs that elevate your soul. Sing to arrange your life well.

It makes sense to suffer and adjust yourself to certain conditions, but only if they elevate you.

The desire for doing good comes from Love, hold to it always; however, you can change the methods for doing good.

What does it mean to love? To love means to serve, to give. Love and do not worry about the consequences.

Master your Love, Wisdom, and Truth without making mistakes the same way the musician masters his skill of playing his instrument. Once he becomes a grand master, he makes no mistakes.

Which man is full of Love? A man whose soul, spirit, mind, and heart are under the full influence of Love.

Love that fulfills the heart only is a short-lived Love.

When Love visits you, you are in the dawn of your life; when it leaves you, you are in the sunset of your life.

Why is man on Earth? To study and learn. To study and learn how to transform his human consciousness into Divine consciousness.

Manifesting patience is manifesting Wisdom. God favors those with patience.

One of the reasons some people suffer is the bad tongue they have. If you have nothing good to say, it'll be better if you keep quiet.

The manifestation of God connects you with Love. Your connection with Love is the most important connection you can have.

Law: If you love people, you are doing good to yourself. If you don't love them, you harm yourself.

Money in Heaven is the goodness you have done on Earth.

The ability to learn, to think, to perform good actions, to love, are great instruments that you must use to get back into Paradise.

What you learn, think, and love matters a lot. There is higher knowledge and there is lower knowledge, there is right thinking and there is wrong thinking, there is Love toward God and there is Love of lower things. You determine where you want to be.

He who wants to be a good student must set right his distorted mind and heart. The good student sets right the distorted trends of his mind and feelings.

Some people get the feeling that they have to do something good for somebody, but they postpone it until the next day. No! The good for today must be made today, tomorrow's good tomorrow.

Your first task is to give way to the positive in yourself. People who give way to the negative in themselves are ill in their minds and hearts. Free your mind from negative thoughts and your heart from negative feelings.

Acquire knowledge; life will show you why you need it.

What will set the world right? Applying Love will set the world right. Many tried the stick, but couldn't do it.

Only Love that comes from God is a real Love. Say, "God is Love and I am in It. In the great name of Love, I can accomplish all of my wishes."

Think about the Divine and accept the Divine in you. Whoever accepts the Divine will easily progress; whoever does not accept it will enter a street with no exit.

If you believe, think, and work, something good will come out of you, but if you don't, nothing good will come out of you.

When one sees his life set right, then he sees the whole world set right. Then he holds his life in his own hands.

In the materialistic world, people look for logic and proof in order to get things clear and understood, and then they believe in them. In the Divine world, the process is the opposite. First comes the belief and then the things become clear to you.

You are rewarded by God when you forgive, not when you retaliate.

With the surplus comes also suffering. You are walking with a bag full of gold, a heavy burden to carry by yourself, and you can hardly take your breath. To make it easy on you, give part of it to the poor. Mother Nature does not bear any extremes, neither extreme surpluses nor extreme privations.

Work on yourself, on your body, to create nice lines on your face and body. Every movement has its meaning. Aspire to harmonic movements.

If you work with the good and lose, do not worry, at the end the loss will transform into gain. This is the belief.

If you do not have a real idea which direction you should go in your life, keep this idea in your mind: study and acquire real knowledge.

Acquiring false teaching is like going to a false doctor, who will direct you to a graveyard with his knowledge.

The most valuable treasure one may have is the knowledge, Wisdom, and Love he has.

The teacher is for this: to deliver knowledge to the student, the student's task in return is to apply it.

Many blame God, why is He not helping them? God helps those who do their best. Help yourself in order for God to help you as well.

Not to pay what you owe means you have no belief. Later you will pay everything with the interest.

The thought of a man has a transforming power. The good, right, nice thought can transform your desperation into a quiet and pleasant condition.

The thought of a man is a magic wand with which you can create miracles. When you lose it, you lose everything.

God will help you after you have tried everything. What is impossible for a man is possible for God.

What would I gain if I believe in and love God? You will gain a lot. Have you ever heard of a singer asking himself what would he gain if he knew how to sing, or a driver what would he gain if he knew how to drive? Should you be asking yourself why would you have to think and act right? If you think and act right, something good will come out of you; if you do not think and act right, nothing good will come out of you.

People become stupid when they ask idols and made-up gods for help. And what do they get from them? They get nothing, and in addition, they lose whatever they have. Pray to the live God, to the great Consciousness, which is perfection.

Find out a great idea in yourself and hold to it. If it endures all tests and conditions, it is a real idea. The true idea you have is your most valuable asset. You can rely on it; nobody can take it away from you.

One must work, not to expect from God or people to do his job. God will help you when you work hard, and when you really need help and you turn to Him for help, He will help you.

If you do not thank Mother Nature every day for everything she gives you, your suffering will be greater.

Put in practice Love, Wisdom, Good, and Truth. The remainder of your life on Earth is not limitless.

Your capital in heaven is the quantity of good you have made on Earth.

How can one set his life right? Simple, remove the elements that spoil it.

It is natural to be good; it is unnatural to be bad. It is wise to manifest goodness and foolish to manifest badness.

Only he loves who relates to others as he relates to himself.

People don't want to understand the good because they have to pay for it. They even do not suspect that that is the best thing they can buy.

The great thing is Love, but greater than that is God's spirit. Love is a fruit of the spirit.

Without Love, one lacks a strong mind, a good heart, and strength. Without Love, one has no good life and no vital strength.

To love is eternal dawn for you. The sunset comes when you throw out the good thoughts from your mind, the good feelings from your heart.

When one prays, he opens his eyes, he lives, and he sees how beautiful the spiritual world is. Whoever does not pray is a "dead" man.

Do this: Be glad when you see some virtue in somebody. Close your eyes when you see something wrong, and ask God to help this man to set it right.

The meaning of life is locked in manifesting Love.

Put Love as a foundation of your home, put Goodness and virtue as a wall, Wisdom as a roof, and Truth as windows.

One thing will save you when you are broke, applying Love!

Many people are slaves to the outer conditions. Apply faith, start loving the whole world, and you will be free.

In the future, the relationships among people must be based on cleanness and holiness. If they keep repeating the contemporary kind of relations among each other, that will be a waste of time.

Knowledge is acquired from higher beings. Do not expect knowledge from ordinary people.

Love that gives way to the ego in you is not Divine. Love that comes from God helps you to develop your talents and stimulates your virtues.

Use natural methods, the good you acquire with them is lasting, artificial methods begin with great effects, but always end up bad for you.

The reason for the badness lies in you. The reason for the goodness lies in you. To transform your bad traits into good is the alive science. When suffering comes upon the wise man, he says, "There is nothing bad in this suffering. It is just another lesson sent from my Father Who loves me and Whom I love to test my Love for Him. In His great name, I will overcome this difficulty."

One of the reasons for evil in man is the food he consumes. Bad food delivers harmful elements in you that affect your mind and behavior. Eat good organic food. Do not eat much, but a little.

Somebody may say, "What for do I need knowledge and Wisdom? I don't need Wisdom; I need money." For the same thing, the mathematician needs formulas to solve a puzzle, the mechanic his tools to fix a car, the doctor medical equipment to diagnose and treat a disease, the firefighter water to distinguish a fire. In the same way, Wisdom is an instrument with which you can overcome your difficulties and problems.

Some people say that they are followers of this Divine teaching, others say, "We are followers of that Divine teaching," but when the time comes, both followers put their guns on set deadly fire against each other. Is this fire from the Divine? The student from a Divine teaching is not allowed to kill his brother. Excuses are easy to find.

One must become used to always being ready to do something good for others, not to be in the habit of using others.

Forgive. Until you learn the law of forgiveness and how to apply it, no science, no formulas, will help you.

To forgive all those who do not love you is every student's task from the Divine teaching. This is how your Love is tested.

Some people spend all of their time thinking about common and ordinary things; no wonder they don't progress much. Others spend half an hour and more thinking about the good, faith, Love, thinking about the great things of the world. These people are cultivating the soil for their future genius.

God's teaching is the best soil; whoever falls on that soil will grow and multiply.

Evil in man is an abnormal condition. It is manifested through weak people. Strengthen your will; do not let your negative traits manifest themselves.

Tell yourself the Truth about your defects and you will free yourself from the restrictions you are living in.

Prepare yourself for paradise. With the burden of materialism, one will not stay a second in paradise. The materialism that a man has in his consciousness is so heavy that if he happens to enter paradise with it, he will be expulsed for less than a second or he will go down.

Arm yourself with Truth, Good, Wisdom, and Love, and begin to erase your sins from the past. Ask for forgiveness and forgive.

If you coerce your neighbor, you coerce God in him; if you coerce yourself, you coerce God in you. With coercing, you do not elevate yourself, but with Love only can you elevate your soul.

Life on Earth is a combination of good and evil, happiness and suffering, Love and hate. The life of a man contains great lessons about good, bad, Love, and hatred, for which he pays dearly. Be glad when you come across evil, be glad when you come across good, be glad that people die, and be glad that people are born. Death comes to change one's old and worn-down cloth with a new one. Evil comes to teach you a lesson.

Holding on to evil thoughts and negative feelings in you will surely bring on you a disaster or disease. By holding on to evil thoughts and negative feelings, you attract the negative powers of the world.

One achieves good results when he works in good disposition of his spirit. Divine consciousness works in man when he is in good disposition.

A thousand years are not enough to achieve something, if you ever achieve something without working with Love.

I ask, "How can you rectify a proud man?" Act with Love with him, nothing more. There is no other power that can soften a man's pride. That's how you will soften it and put it in its normal condition.

In man's life where Love does not reign there, greed will be born.

Christ says, "I am the Way, the Truth, and the Life." I am that way that teaches people how to act. I am the Truth that teaches people how to love. I am the Life that teaches people how to think. "I am the Way, the Truth, and the Life." When you enter this way, you will act well, you will work well. And when you enter the Truth, you cannot stay indifferent, you will love all people! This is the Truth! And when you enter Life, you will think together with all people and you will take the nice from them from everywhere. Such interpretations these words and ideas have. That's how Christ understood it.

Every man who spontaneously performs good actions, he is one of us.

I am teaching you the nicest thing: "Learn to love God!" This is Love!

So I am telling you now if you are listening to me, according to the Law of Love, you will understand these things. With Love, all things have meaning. In Wisdom, all things have meaning. And in Truth, all things have meaning. **Outside of God rests the meaningless of life.** There hell is, there the mishap is, and there the muddle is. We have to strive for God to come and live in us.

Which are the signs of Love? Patience and kindness, according to Apostle Paul. Passage: 1 Corinthians 13.

Love is manifested through the law of Wisdom. Wisdom is manifested through the law of Truth. Truth is realized in life. It is a circle. You have to be reasonable in order to enter Love and to benefit from all that it caries.

The Master about music:
Music is an urge for life. One cannot become noble if he does not sing and play a musical instrument. Otherwise, he will remain rude or an "unpolished stone."

Do not hide from yourself your mistakes. Confess them so that you can rectify them. Each and every mistake that you keep in your consciousness, rectify it. Every mistake that is before your consciousness, before your mind, heart, soul, and spirit, you will be able to overcome and then you will be able to free yourself from one evil. If you hide the mistake, you will do yourself an evil.

The human heart can be rectified only through studying and serving.

Do to others that what you want others to do for you.

There is nothing nicer than Love.
There is nothing lighter and brighter than Wisdom.
There is nothing wider than Truth.
Truth is the whole eternity. It has no borders. When you enter Wisdom, there everything is light and bright, everything is clean. When you enter Love, there life is peace, joy, all these things are there. So I am telling you, learn to serve God with all of your heart. This is the way without exception, for the righteous, and for the genius, and for the gifted, for all!

If you are in insubordination, in contradiction with Love, suffering will come. If you are in contradiction with Wisdom, suffering will come. If you are in contradiction with the Truth, suffering will come. That is how the law is. For whoever it may be, it is like that!

As soon as you put economies on your Love, it is all gone! Love does not bear any economies! You say, "Wait, I will love this one like this, that one like that!" No, give everyone for free, give everyone in abundance, and do not put any economies into the Love.

Remember these three things: Know people and love people! Know God and love God! Know yourself and love yourself!

Love one another! Even in the worst conditions, why shouldn't you come to an agreement?

As students, you have to have one thing: You have to have respect and honor for one another. Because when you respect others, you respect yourself. When you love others, you love yourself. Always direct your mind to God and say, "Lord, teach me to love people as you love them; teach me to know people as you know them, and teach me to act as you act."

The basic reason for all things is the spirit. The first result of the spirit in the world, the first result in the world with which life begins, that is Love. The result of Love is the life on Earth. The life that we have is a result.

In order to love somebody, you have to be ready to get in his situation and he has to be ready to get in your situation too. A king must get in the situation of his citizens and vice versa.

Love is not the easiest science. You, when you enter Love, you will be absolutely free. You will enter one completely new world. When you enter Love, no memory will remain in you about your suffering. You will look at all of your life, and you will see that in everything is hidden something nice.

The only thing that frees man is Love. Knowledge and freedom are the ways through which Love is manifested. Freedom is in the physical world, knowledge is in the spiritual world, and Love is in the Divine world. Love itself is the manifestation of God's spirit, something deeper.

In our lives, we are constantly tested how far our Love has reached. The whole of life and the suffering are a constant test on us from the invisible world where we have come with our Love.

You all have to have right thought. God absolutely dislikes any white lies, absolutely dislikes anything unclean.

In nature, friction between good people is absolutely forbidden.

The scripture says, "Defeat evil with good." I say in other words: "Leave good to deal with evil in the world. Don't get in direct contact with evil." The scripture says, "Do not resist evil." It means: Do not engage with evil to fight it.

I talk about Love as a science so you can acquire life. I am not talking about ordinary life, about temporary Love. For me, the great law from which can be acquired eternal life is important when I talk about Love.
The scripture says, "This is eternal life: to know You, the only God of love." From that emerges life. Then I talk about Wisdom, because life can be supported only with knowledge. If a man has life, he cannot acquire eternal life if he does not have Divine Wisdom in himself. These acquired riches he cannot keep and cannot develop without Divine Wisdom. So I say Love is a science that you must study.

When one loves you, he loves you because you have the image of the Divine, because the Divine brings Love. Love is Love because it brings life. Love that brings no life is not Love.

I tell you all: Be smart! Apply Love as a science. The powers of Love must be studied.

You have to have very wide views. If you do the will of God, you will live. You cannot elevate yourself if you do not do the will of God.

I want God's work to be done. If I do the work of God, I am on the right path. You all have to do God's work as much as you can, little by little.

The essence of life, that is Love, because into Love are hidden the conditions of life. You have to be interested in Love because all conditions, all riches of life, emerge from Love. Knowledge or Wisdom is needed because it is a world from which emerge the riches of your thought. If you don't have thought, you don't have conditions, and you cannot progress. Or the wealth of Truth that is in the world of freedom. You cannot be free if you are not acquainted with the world of Truth. Somebody will ask, "What thing is the absolute Truth?" Truth cannot be absolute. Facts can be absolute. Truth is Truth, you cannot make comparisons. That this is Truth and that is more Truth; it cannot be spoken like that.

In the Divine world, everything is possible. There is nothing impossible. Put in your mind: Everything is possible, you can achieve anything. Believe in it and it will happen.

There is a law. They say, "We have to believe in God, because if you do not believe in God, you will remain a first-class fool; if you do not believe in God, you will remain a first-class poor man. If you do not believe in God, you will never be healthy."

Become smart, become healthy, and become rich. Three things. Any teaching that does not provide these things is not a true teaching. Every teaching must have thought, healthfulness, and riches.

In order for a genius to be born in the world, every morning to that pregnant woman must be played the best musical pieces. To that genius, through the music we will bring in all gifts and you will give conditions for all talents to develop. At least once should a nice piece of music be played, so she can start thinking. Music makes man think.

What thing is the bad man? The bad man is everyone who lives for himself only. He wants all conditions to cooperate for his own good.

Man is strong till he thinks. If you want to be strong, you have to think. When you think, you are in connection with the other world, the world beyond, from which they can help you. A man who thinks is always helped. A man who does not think never gets helped.

A man is strong when good reigns in him. A man is strong when Love reigns in him. A man is strong when Truth reigns in him. Three things must reign. When you become strong, acknowledge the power of Love. Then you are a strong man. To become strong, you have to acknowledge the power of Wisdom, then you are strong man. To become strong, you have to acknowledge the power of Truth, then you are a strong man.

Love brings health. Love brings freedom. Love brings life. Even if you are dead when Love comes, it will bring you back to life.

Love resurrects the dead. Love lifts up the sick. Love enriches the poor. Love enlightens the ignorant. It does everything.

The new teaching will be the teaching of Love. The new teaching will be a teaching of knowledge, of light. The new teaching will be a teaching of freedom, to give you freedom. If you meet a smart man, listen to him. The one who is ignorant should listen to the one who is smart. The strong one should help the one who is weak.

You ask: What is God's Love? He has made the world. That is one good benefit. Make use of that world. The goodness, that you use, the life that you have, our thoughts, our feelings, all of this is manifested in God's Love. If we are blind to this, then in what else will Love get manifested?

I wish you God's Love to be your Love, and your Love to be God's Love. That means to have harmony with the great in the world we have to become conductors of God's Love.

If you love somebody, you develop yourself. It is a privilege for you.

That which comes easy, easy goes. Those things that you have acquired or achieved with great difficulties, they will remain valuable for you. Know that one day in your life will remain only the great things. The easy things are generally handy for everyone. If you want something valuable to remain in your life, to bring you joy, those are the greatest difficulties. So I say: Suffering will leave in you the most valuable things.

For me, everyone is young who has pure mind, pure heart, and pure deeds.

Real in life is only that which no one can take away from you. Everything that they can take away is to show you that those things are not real, they are an illusion. Consequently, your worries should be temporary.

There is one Love that connects people. When you get acquainted with that Love, that Love is the reality of life. That Love I call Love of God. Love, which unites all people, brings meaning to life, brings meaning to all deeds. That Love I call Love of God or Love toward all souls. It is one. Now you may ask the question: "Is it possible to love all people?" With present-day Love, it is impossible.

You cannot have faith until you begin to love. In order to boost your faith, you have to have Love. Without Love, one's faith cannot be strengthened. Love raises faith. The one whom you love, in him you believe more. The one whom you don't love, in him you believe less.

I preach Love based on this law. I want to boost people's faith. But faith cannot be boosted if you do not have Love as its subject. When Love becomes the subject, Faith gets boosted.

You say, "I cannot love this man." **What you say is wrong.** Then put in your mind: You can love everyone whom God has created. Everyone whom God has created I can love. Everyone whom people have created I'll think about it. But put a definite idea in your mind: Every man whom God has created, every man who has a soul, I can love. Everyone who has spirit I can love; everyone who has mind I can love. Everyone who has heart I can love. If he has those things, they are Divine. When he comes, you will accept him. It is the new thought that you have to have.

I have told you before that in God there are two wills. If you go by the law of good, you will try God's goodwill; if you go by the law of evil, you will try God's evil will. If you want to go both ways, you cannot expect the same results.

Never think that you are something higher than other people because higher from all is only God. If you love somebody who sits higher than you, you will become like him. If you love somebody who is lower than you, you will become like him. Love always makes people alike. The one you love like him you will become.

I keep one rule. I always look after the following: If a thought is right, from whomever it has emerged, apply it. If a thought is wrong, from whomever it may have emerged, do not apply it. Nothing more.

Why do you have to love? If you do not love, you cannot achieve that what you want. And if you love and you are loved, you can achieve that what you want. If you are not loved and you do not love, you cannot achieve that what you want. This is now that language of Love. Love is a method for achieving in the present life that to whatever our soul aspires.

Think about that which you have never thought before. Do not think about ordinary things. Think about this which you have never thought about. Remember, today's thought is this, that Love, Wisdom, Truth, life, knowledge, freedom, everything, is an opportunity that when applied, one can achieve everything, and he will be glad and joyful. He will be joyful in God and God will be joyful in him.

Formula: Say it three times:
The way of the righteous is a way of dawning.

Now, real in the world is Love. Real in the world is Virtue. The ideal is Wisdom. The ideal is the knowledge that you acquire.

If you hate somebody, he will hate you too. So whatever you give him, he will pay you back with the same. If you love somebody, he will love you too.

Love is generosity.

Hatred is miserliness. There is a similarity between hatred and miserliness.

Every hate comes from the fact that somebody had wronged you, he has taken something from you, has done some harm to you. He has deprived you of something. Love is the opposite. All people who have given us something we are inclined to love. You ask how to love? Start giving! When you love somebody, you have to give him something. You cannot give to anybody if you do not love him. And if you do not give to anybody, he cannot love you. You say, "Why should I love him? And why should he love me?" When I love, I have sown the field. That is Love. And when he loves me, it means that the field has produced wheat. He who understands that will love you in return.

When you love somebody, that thought and feeling will give birth to a fruit in him, and you will reap a crop, and then there will be a reverse Love.

Now you want without loving to be loved. That in no way can happen.

I say, if you have loved, expect to be loved. If you have not loved, love! If you have been loved, love so there can be repayment, so you can pay back. There must be repayment, an exchange in nature. If you stop that exchange, if there is no exchange, the mishaps will start coming.

It is said, "Christ came on Earth to show the Love that God gave Him." We have to show that Love that Christ has given us.

To show God's Love, Christ had to bear the sins of the people to stand such suffering that only a few could bear.

Love gives everything and takes everything. It gives a lot and takes a lot. When it gives a little, it takes a little, keep that in mind.

Your heart to be occupied with Love constantly! Your mind to be always occupied with Wisdom, and you as students to be always occupied with the Truth!

That one who has comprehension of Love, nothing in the world can disturb him. For as long as you are getting disturbed in life, for so long you do not have a true understanding of Love, you have Love, but that is not God's Love.

I say: Start studying the laws of Love. That person whom God has sent to you, show him your Love. When he leaves, he will glorify God. He will say: "Blessed is the hour in which I met this man. He dressed me with something."

Turn to God with all the contradiction that you meet in your life, but with Love.

Love makes a man's soul free. Love dresses the soul with a bright dress. Love dresses the man's soul with life. When Love comes, it will dress you with life, it will give you light, and it will give you freedom. Where there is life, light, knowledge, and freedom, there is Love.

Music is a great law that determines the direction of one's thoughts, the direction of one's feelings, and the direction of one's actions.

Everything nice and beautiful in life is determined by the great law of music. If you are not a musical person, you cannot achieve anything.

Till then, till we learn how to love, we are in the world of dependence, and happy people we cannot be. Love is the way for one's happiness.

This that must remain in your mind is the following: The road to man's happiness is Virtue. The opportunity for Virtue is Divine Love. This is what you have to know in your present life. The road to virtue is the road for your happiness, and to achieve your happiness, it is Love that will provide the opportunity. Virtue is the way, but Love is one of the opportunities, and if you don't have that opportunity, you cannot have the way, because virtue has emerged from Love. So, each one of you must know whether you go on the road of virtue. This must be determined in your conscience. Is your road a way of virtue?

You want to become a musician. Only through the way of virtue and Love can you become one. You want to become beautiful, rich, and strong. Whatever you may want in the world, the way must be virtue, but to have an opportunity, you have to have Love.

Patience is a great power in man. It is necessary, it does not matter what you are—an angel, a man, or an animal—patience is a necessity. It is one of God's great qualities. It is said that God's patience is a long lasting one. All social issues cannot be arranged in any other way except by the law of Divine Love. Only Love is in the condition to arrange things.

If you marry without Love, you are committing a crime. That's how it is from the Divine viewpoint. When you marry without Love, you are not in consideration with yourself and you are not in consideration with God. You are lying to yourself and God! And if you give birth to children and you don't love them, then you are lying to yourself and God.

I will give you one rule for those who will be getting married now. Those who are married they have broken the rule, but those who will be getting married now for them is this rule: Never tell to your beloved not even a single insulting word, neither verbally, neither in writing, neither in thinking, neither with feeling. You will think that whatever he does is right, that it cannot be more right.

Faith: Faith is connected with one's mind. If you do not understand your mind, you have weak faith. Firstly, I evaluate one's faith according to his mind. The more the mind is developed, the stronger the faith. The less the mind is developed, the weaker the faith.

Faith is a capital that no one can rob. The man of faith I liken to a giant spring from which even if thousands of people take water with barrels they still can't empty. Develop your faith. Don't settle with knowing how Christ talked, but know how He lived as well. Did Christ complain? Back then he was persecuted. Many Jewish rabbis were saying that the Christ teaching was not the Moses teaching, that it was a backward one. They were saying, "Moses taught an eye for an eye, and if you get slapped once, you slap twice," but this One says, "If they take your cloak, give them your shirt as well."

A Christian who is walking on the new road must be generous! You have to be generous.

Breathing:
When you inhale, say, "Lord, I accept your Love in me."
When you exhale, say, "Lord, this light that you gave me I send it to other people so you can be glorified." This is breathing!

Christ says, "Love your enemies." And we say, "Do you love your enemies? You have loved your father, your brothers, and your sisters. The ideal to love your enemies is a very heavy ideal. Some say that they can love their enemies. You try it."

Say: "Things will be OK!" Why will things be OK? Because God created the world. If you study, things definitely will be OK.

I am telling you three things: Put Love in your heart, put Wisdom in your mind, and put the Truth in your will and your body, the Truth to live in your body. Your body, everything in you, should get connected with the Truth, so the Truth may express the beauty.

When you make a mistake, thank God that you have not made a bigger mistake. And when you perform good actions, make a wish from God to perform better actions the next time.

When you perform good actions, rejoice and make a wish for your good actions to increase. But when you make a mistake, make a wish next time for your mistake to be twice as small. The mistake cannot be reduced all at once, but gradually. Regarding the good you perform, make a wish to increase it gradually as well. This is what you have to be wishing now.

Remember one rule: When you want an indulgence to get satisfied, that indulgence breaks the man's freedom. Whoever serves indulgence, he breaks his own freedom. He breaks not just his own freedom, but the freedom of the others as well. To indulge yourself, that must be the last thing in your life. If you want at the very first to indulge yourself, you will get in trouble.

The desire to love is a Divine impulse. When and how, who and how much you will give, are up to your disposition. That you have to love everybody, it is from the Divine.

"Why was I born a woman"? I will answer you. "So you can learn the freedom that is contained in Love. The man asks: "Why was I born a man?" So you can learn the light that is contained in Wisdom.
"Why am I a child?" So you can learn the freedom of the Truth. I say: To such is the kingdom of God, to the children. We have to become children so we can learn the freedom of the Truth.

The righteous man is that one who in all of his actions acts the same. So he has a Divine measurement in himself. He measures himself and his neighbor with one and the same measurement.

Can a man be righteous? Without Love, man cannot be righteous. Righteousness has Love as an impulse. Righteousness starts from Love. If you want to be righteous, only Love can give it to you.
But good without Wisdom you cannot be.

In order for one to be good, Wisdom must come.

From God has come the spirit; from the spirit has come Love.

In Love, in life, one must always act fairly. That is how God acts.

If God does not come in you, if His spirit does not come, if Love does not come in you, then good and fair you cannot be. Without Love in the world, there is no fairness or justice. Without Wisdom, there is no goodness.

We say: God is Love, God is Wisdom, and God is Truth. In other words, Love, Wisdom, and Truth comprise the three fundamental things through which God is manifested. Between Love, Wisdom, and Truth, nothing else can get in. If you have Love, if you have Wisdom, if you have Truth, they are the only reality that you can count on. Nothing can get in among them; nothing can split them. You can build with them now everywhere. Wherever you go, they do not lose their value, their power, and their good. And they never lose their fairness or justice.

We are seeking that Love, that Wisdom, that power in the world that must rejuvenate us, that must resurrect us, to bring us back to life, to make us smart, good, and strong, that's what we seek.

Everything that we have lost so far we can find in only three ways: through the road of Love, the road of Wisdom, and the road of Truth. Those are the ways.

What is the meaning of life? The meaning of life is the Truth. Then comes the question, what is the Truth?" That which connects all things in one unity and gives them meaning that is the Truth. There is nothing else behind the Truth. Behind the Truth exists a disorganized world in which a human foot can never step.

Happiness outside of God you cannot have.

Coming out of God is sorrow. Returning back to God is joy. When you come back to God, you feel restriction, and you want to free yourself. You come out of God, you free yourself, but the sorrow comes.

Now many of you think that when you go to God, you will be absolutely free. To be absolutely free, you have to merge with God. You should not think for yourself. Till you think for yourself you are not free. Because then you and God are different things.
Truth is that great law or that essence that frees man from all contradictions.

Truth is that great law that shows us the ways of Love.

The wish of Love is to give us life. The wish of Wisdom is to give us light and knowledge. The wish of Truth is to give us freedom. But freedom is the fruit. It is that which will bring meaning to life.

If you don't sacrifice yourself for others, others can't sacrifice themselves for you. If you can't love, others can't love you. If you can't think about others, others cannot think about you.

God has given us larynx, one soft pellicle on which He wrote, "God is Love," and whoever pronounces every day those words well and harmonically, everything will start going well in his life.

Without love of God, you cannot become good. Until the moment you realize that you have been born and come out of God, and consequently have relations with Him, you cannot become good. You have to realize that you have come out of God and everything that He has given you, you have to use for God. Then you love Him. God has sent you to Earth and He loves you.

Firstly, try the Divine thoughts, learn to apply them. Without that, there is no success in life. As much as you perceive the Divine thoughts in yourself, so much your progress will be, so much your health will be, and so smart you will be. And all of your life will be determined by that situation of the Divine thoughts you have perceived in yourself. That is as much true and correct as whatever you eat such you will become.

All of your physical life is determined by the food that you accept. All your human life is determined by those Divine thoughts that you will perceive.

If you perceive a single Divine thought in yourself, it is worth not a million, but billions. In the future, it will be a tremendous fortune.

If you want honor from people, honor them. If you want Love from people, love them.

Think about God every day. Not about what He is. Just think about Him, because when you do, something nice will come in you. Just think of the Lord. He is the best. He is the image of Love, like the sun that rises. Do not think that He will judge you. If you remember Him every day, right away something will come in you that will stimulate your heart. After your heart gets stimulated, then your mind, your soul, and your strength will get stimulated.

If I cannot be patient with others, I harm myself.

You have painted a picture. Critique the picture, but not yourself. Do not critique your gift! Make another picture and correct yourself. You can correct and critique each and every action of yours, but of yourself never say, "I am an ungifted man" or "I am a bad man." You can say, "My deed could be bad in that particular case, but I am not bad. The picture may not be good, but that does not show that I am ungifted. I just have not paid enough attention."

God has put in your heart all conditions for a better life and purity. A man's heart must be manifested. The good that is in man must be manifested, and that good can only be manifested through the heart. The Law of Love begins with the heart. And if you cannot get born with your heart, you won't be able to with your mind either.

The scripture says, "Pray for each other." Wish one another nice things. When you see somebody, pray for his gift to strengthen, the one who got rich to get richer.

Good is harmony, but evil disharmony. Anyone who is not good will be unhappy, as unhappiness is a state of being disorganized.

Good will show you the road to God. When you find God, He will show you how to love people. In order to find God, you need to love Him.

Love supports the good. The good supports richness.

The more remorse you feel and the more you rejoice, the better you will become. The better you become, the nearer to Love you will be. And the nearer to Love you are, the better you will serve God. This is the road on which we all must walk. This is the road on which we all must be diligent. This is the road of human development.

Now on what does one's happiness depend? Man's happiness depends on his well-organized mind, on his well-organized heart, and on his well-organized will.

Man's strength sits in his reasonableness. If you are reasonable, you will have strength. If you are not reasonable, you won't have strength in yourself. All things in the world happen with strength.

You say that you have Love of God, but you get offended easily. The one who has Love of God is deaf for the bad things. Whatever bad thing he is told, he does not hear it. For his Love of God, he is ready to bare anything. People who are in love are patient and prudent. The world suffers from that which it is not in love with something lofty.

Love is a reasonable power. If you with your spirit do not love God, you won't have strength in yourself.

That for which people can honor you are your soul, your spirit, your mind, and your heart. All other things in the world have emerged from these four powers in man. These are treasures that we have to study. If you don't study the treasures of your heart, your mind, your soul, and your spirit, you will never find happiness.

Man's strength does not sit in that what people give him, because that what people give they may take back, even on Easter. Man's strength sits in the Love he shows. Strong is that one who shows his Love, but not the one to whom Love is shown. Strong is God, because He shows His Love. He has created the world and does not need anything. He tells the people: "If you want to be happy, you have to show your Love."

How is Love defined? Love is defined in the following way. The only thing in the world that does not lose faith is Love. The only thing in the world that does not lose hope is Love. Consequently, faith and hope are absolute in Love. He who has Love in himself easily copes with anything and everything.

We have to think on how to do the will of God. We have come on Earth to do God's will. Man's faith, his greatness, lies in doing God's will. We have to bare three things in mind. The first thing is to be holy in the name of God, to forget about everything that is related to us. The second thing is with all of our heart, mind, and soul to wish for the kingdom of God on Earth. And the third thing is with our very being to wish for the will of God to be fulfilled on Earth.

Love is a law of variety. Love infers limitless happiness in which the universe is immersed. You are living in the world, but you have closed your mind and your heart, but you have to know that God's goods are received namely through the mind and the heart. How will happiness come for you if your mind and your heart are closed? Every day in your mind must shine one bright thought; every day in your heart must shine one warm feeling.

Children have excellent and uncorrupted minds and hearts, consequently, all those people who possess uncorrupted minds and hearts are children of God. To them belongs the Kingdom of God.

The new sits in the following: Your mind and your heart must become like those of children. Then you have to start to serve God with Love

There is nothing impossible for God. When somebody says that he is a sinner that means he does not love. As soon as he begins to love, he will right away become righteous. "But I am not a happy man." You are unhappy because you do not love. When you begin to love, you will be happy. "I am poor." You are poor because you do not love. When you begin to love, you will become a rich person. "I am an ignorant man." You are ignorant because you do not love. Start loving and you will become a learned man. The Love that brings all the goods in the world can develop all the capabilities and feelings of a man.

When Love comes in man, he will resurrect.

Why does suffering come? Suffering comes so you can know the Lord. When you turn to Him, He heals you and tells you: "I don't want you to be such self-willed children."

In man is deposited a great treasure about which he doesn't even suspect. He must start working upon that treasure. When one does not know the valuables of his mind, of his heart, of his soul and his spirit, he does not know anything.

I say: Begin with putting into practice becoming strong and living right. Stop living only for yourself. If you do not live only for yourself, you will have everything. The whole world suffers from that, that it does not love God. Now from everyone is required Love of God. That Love includes the good for all the people of the world.

When people love one another, their things get arranged very easily.

Always pay respect to one another. Study that, what God has deposited in you. Apply Love toward every living thing in the world. In that way, all of your difficulties that are tormenting you will get resolved.

Under "Love," we understand the manifestation of God.

What is Love? Love gives. You, when you love, you have to give.

When you tell somebody "I love you," you will feel that more life has come in you. And every person who tells you "I love you" has put life in you. But anyone who does not tell you "I love you" has taken something from you.

What is Love? Love gives life.

Knowledge is that which gives power to man. Knowledge that does not carry power in itself is not knowledge.

Wisdom brings power.

If you do not love God, you will get old. Why should we love God? You will love God to rejuvenate yourself. You will love God to become young. You will love God to feed yourself well. You will love God to become smart. All these great goods in life come from the Love of God. The Love of God is the solution of the issues. The Love of God is a process of renovation and renewal. What is Love? A process of renewal.

The other world, the world beyond, is a world of purity. Man's opportunities lie in purity. The good life lies in purity. Where there is impurity, it always brings suffering. Disharmony brings suffering too. But harmony, purity, fairness, meekness, abstention and self-restrain, they are the qualities that bring great goods.

I say: The world needs conductors of Love, the Divine and reasonable one. Man must be a conductor. Do you know what it means for a man to be a conductor? For a man to be a conductor, he must have that faith that a child has. Mothers take their children to pray for rain. One kid took an umbrella in his hand. His mother asked him: "Why did you take that umbrella?" The child replied, "Because it will rain." The mother said, "Maybe it will rain, maybe it will not." Now we pray and say: "Maybe it will happen, maybe it won't." We have to have that children's belief that it will be.

There is a law in nature that says: Every thought, every feeling, and every deed cannot go without producing their consequences. And that what we think one day will come to us. So the first thing is: Strive to be set right in your soul, be fair. Man must be fully fair.

Do not preach something that you have not tried.

The hardest art for a man in the world is to be patient because in patience are interweaved all the contradictions of life.

All people suffer so they can learn, because if they do not suffer, they won't learn.

God wants to take off from us those pretentious views that we have so we can be left with the essence that we need.

We suffer from the great abundance. God has given us everything, but we have left it without working on it. We, with the great richness that we have, expect more richness to come to us. So I say, the richness that is in us, work on it.

On Sunday, while walking through town, you are asking yourself: "How to preach?" When you pass by somebody, tell him very kindly, "Very nice day, we have an excellent day," and walk on. These words will remain in his mind. Or tell him, "Good day or good afternoon, a great good is coming for the world," and walk on. Put these positive thoughts in him. There are a lot of other things that can be said.

THE SUCCESS OF A MAN DEPENDS ON HIS FAITH: HIS FAITH IN GOD, HIS NEIGHBOR AND HIMSELF.

Be glad when you meet a smart man, he is a blessing for you.

What is Love? Love is that longing in which, as you live, you will get the achievement you have the desire for.

There are countless abilities in man's soul, because it is the expression of God Himself. The soul is made of the image and likeness of God.

One cannot understand the things until he tries them.

You say: "I believe in God." Firstly, think about God, then you will feel God. You have to become a servant of God; you have to do something for Him. If you have a Lord for whom you have not thought the best, if you have not put Him in yourself to think the best, to have the best feelings, to do good things for Him, to do favors for others, you cannot know God.

The name we have for God is not the true one, because if we know His true name, it will get stained. The one who pronounces the name of God must possess pure heart and deeds. When you pronounce the name of God, pronounce it with that Love, faith, and hope as if God is something great.

In Love, there are no difficulties.
In Love, there is no suffering.
In Love, there are no misunderstandings.
In Love, everything renews.
In Love, there is eternal bliss.

I say: Love is a nice world where I can rest; in Love is paradise.

Love is this that rectifies all mistakes. For me, Love is this that resurrects the people, this that makes them live better and without lying to each other. The nicest and the most beautiful thing is Love. Wherever we see the nice and the beautiful, there Love is. This that is not Love leave it on the side. Allow Love to start acting in you where it has not acted so far.

The words "I cannot do it" in Love do not exist. You will put the words: "I can do it."

The Love in you must bring in its fruit. The Love that you have will always come back to you. Your Love must always go out, do good, and then come back to you. Until it does the whole good, it won't come back to you, and when it comes back, you will be glad.

I say: Put now in your mind the thought, "We have to serve God and we have to serve Love."

What are we going to do for the Lord today? One microscopic good.

The Divine world is an eternal harmony. The outer side of the harmony we call music. The music we consider fun.

Man must be merry. He must see the nice in everything.

Learn to be free! Without Love, there is no freedom. Showing Love right, that is freedom.

Firstly, strive to be free and encourage freedom. Do not limit the freedom! Freedom is the expression of Love. Do not limit the freedom in which Love is manifested. The constant limitation is the reason for all evil.

The spirit has connection with musicality. The good man is musical. The smart man is musical. The strong man is musical. Everything nice and beautiful is connected with music.

Everything that is done without Love has no warmth. Everything that is done with Love has warmth. Love is that which brings warmth.

If your Love and your knowledge cannot deposit in you the law of self-sacrifice, you have not understood what Love is.

Do not think that when you love people you will lose something. Do not think that when you give away Wisdom you will lose. No, you will always win.

All negative thoughts create poisons in you. Firstly, we need to learn to think right so we can free ourselves from the contemporary poisons. Then we say we have to live with Love. But with Love can live only that one who loves God.

One must study the Divine Love. Never eat that which you don't love. The good meal is that one that you love, not the one that people praise. Eat only that which you love, never what you don't.
That is one of the hygienic rules.

Wherever you go, Love should be for you the stimulating (motivating) reason.

When you do a good deed, Christ has come. When you show a nice feeling, Christ has come. When you show a nice thought, Christ has come.

When out of Love you think, feel, and act well, Christ will come. There is nothing nicer than that. Christ is the old brother, the first brother, the best brother people have. The best brother humanity has had is Christ. Who is God? The best father. The best father is God; the best brother is Christ. When He comes, He will bring us Love. He is our father. When He shows Himself, He brings Love. That is how you will know Him.

Whoever eats quickly suffers quickly. Eat slowly and think that in that given case, you are in front of God.

The Lord is everywhere and everything lives and moves in Him. His spirit is in everything.

Never make a judgment to tell somebody, "You do not have Divine Love." Be silent on that issue.

Never leave a bad thought to work in your consciousness. Leave only the positive ones to work. In the evening, review the bill of your life, and do not leave any bad thought to work in your consciousness, because that bad thought will stop your progress and it will do a mischief to you and others as well.

It is necessary for a man to forget about himself, to become a servant of the Lord, and to start thinking about the Lord.

When Love comes, the evil will disappear by itself.

We have to love each other. Love is the greatest good. Love is the greatest means for achievement.

Everyone must pass through the law of Love. Understand Love as an achievement.

I say: Believe that you are good, stop thinking that you are very bad people.

Start to believe that it is not only you who is good, but that others are good too.

Suffering is a method that opens the way for you to enter the Divine world, to enter paradise, and be among the saints and the good people.

There is a law: This that you want for yourself want for all people. Then you will be free. Do not want all people to be like you. Want for them to have knowledge. Want for them to have freedom as you would for yourself. As much as freedom is good for you, it is good for them.

Things that are caused by fear are not Divine. Those things are animal conditions. Divine is this on which Love is the stimulating (motivating) cause.

Every thought that you send out to thank God will come back to you, and will be a blessing for you.

Prana is the power in the world that fills out the space. It exists in potential and kinetic conditions. When it gets interweaved, material forms are shaped.

Never compare yourself with other people. Because if you say, "I know more than him," someone else will say, "I know more than you." Thus, nothing can get accomplished. Do not compare yourself with other people. Consider that everyone knows as much as you do.

With Love, we are dressed up, and without it, we are naked.
What is Love? This that dresses up man.
What is Love? This that feeds man.
What is Love? This that gives power.
What is Love? This that pacifies man.
All those nice things are Love.

There are three channels in man's spine. Two of them are open and through them people breathe. In those channels, flow currents. Up in the big brain and in the sympathetic nervous system, there is a third channel; that channel is the channel of Truth, which in contemporary people is closed. Always note the good in others because it is your good as well. When other people perform good actions, their good enters you.

Paradise is a place where everything is done with Love. You do something with Love and you get paid with Love.

I am against hard work, because it corrupts people. Man must make a living, but unneeded labor is no good, and not to work at all is no good either.

Begin to study Love because without it things have no meaning. Love knowledge as well. You have to study.

MAN IS THAT ONE WHO KNOWS HOW TO LOVE.
MAN IS THAT ONE WHO KNOWS HOW TO STUDY.
MAN IS THAT ONE WHO SEEKS FREEDOM.

Life is tough when one lacks knowledge. Life is tough when a man is not free.

The power of the Christian, the power of the man of the new teaching, sits in that to rectify the mistakes he has made.

When we decide to do something for God, He will help us.

You want to know which faith in the world is the right one. The faith that brings light is the right one.
The faith that brings power is the right one.
When one makes a mistake, contemporary people say, "You did no good." The new philosophy says, "You saw somebody who stole something; whatever he stole, you go and put it in its place. You who saw the theft deliver the person from evil so he does not suffer from it at all."

We want to know which the law of Love is.
Love God so you can be loved.
Do good so you can be loved.

You have to know that you have come on Earth to serve. You also must know that you have come to study Love.

Do not allow in your mind any lie.

Hold on to Love; in it are all opportunities. When you have Love, your mind will be developing right and afterward your actions will be right.

If God is not in the good, if God is not in the right, if God is not in Love, if God is not in Wisdom, if God is not in Truth, if God is not in freedom, and if God is not in life, then where is He?

You cannot live well if you do not think right.

Let there remain in you the idea that God is limitless, kind, gentle, and good.

You cannot become rich if you do not suffer. For all the things that you want to achieve, there is suffering, through which you have to go. Suffering is the soil in which things are sown.

Sometimes you ask, "Why is there suffering?" Without suffering, nothing can be achieved. You ask, "Then where is the Lord?" Suffering is Love's right hand. The Lord has allowed suffering so that the heart, the mind, man's power, and all human virtues can be shown.

In order for a man to become strong, he must first cope with suffering. Evaluate suffering as a method for elevating one's soul. When Christ's students began to understand suffering, they started to enjoy it. The apostles, who at the beginning were crying from suffering, then after being taught by Christ for awhile, were coming back with great joy. For that, for serving God, they had been honored to be beaten.

In suffering, God is present. When we suffer, we are doing work for God. If you want the Lord to visit you, bear the suffering, and work for the Lord. He is there and sees your works. If you do not suffer, it means God knows that you are not working. If you go in the world beyond, you will see that your life will be evaluated by the suffering you have had. To study means to suffer.

So far you have not understood the main thing. You want to understand Love without suffering. Love without suffering cannot be understood.

Whoever says he is happy he loves.

All the time when a man loves, he is happy.
All the time when you do not love, you are not happy.

In Love there is eternal growth.
There is no better condition than Love.

Everyone who does not love is condemned to death. Everyone who loves is blessed to have life. In Love is the blessing of God, but in lovelessness is death.

In what does the new teaching rest? In the Love that carries with itself fairness, honesty, purity, and selflessness.

Everyone who loves God and his neighbors is one of us. Whether they are here or somewhere else, they are one of us.

"How should we love?" The way you want to be loved is how you will love, nothing more.

What does the Lord want from you now? To love your neighbor who has come out from Him. Man's soul has come out of God. Consequently, love that soul.

The one who praises you does good to himself; the one who reproaches you does evil and bad to himself.

In order for compassion and all the other virtues to come, Love must come.

Without Love, you will have the negative side of life.

I preach knowledge as a Divine blessing. Let's study so we can have the blessing of God.
We will love so we can have God's blessing.
We will speak the Truth so we can have God's blessing. Whether people will love me is another issue. To love me or not is their business.

Your happiness depends on the Love of God that you have. Not from the Love that you have for me, nor your Love for your neighbor. From the Love of God that you have depends your future. The Love that you have for others is secondary.

Until we realize that we have only one Father, we cannot set ourselves right in the world. Till we have many fathers, we cannot rectify ourselves. We have to think that we have one Father, that the other fathers are just rays of that Father, God. All fathers who came out of God must acknowledge Him. All mothers, all masters (rulers), all teachers, all must say, "We have one Father; I am not the father."

Think upon this sentence: The God of Love is the way of life.

Feel the presence of God everywhere.

This wave, this teaching, must be passed on everywhere. The new way, this is the way of Love.

The greatest wealth that man carries is life. Life is wealth. All other things are just appliances or adornments of life itself; they are conditions only.

Richness lies in the irresistible faith in God that we have, in the best meaning of it, in that one who gave us life. When we wake up in the morning, there is nothing better for us than this, to think what a great richness it is to think about God.

In singing, you have to feel pleasure in yourself. Sing to yourself first. If you are pleased, you sing well.

When you wake up in the morning, start singing. I wish that you all are singers.

True suffering is temporary. Suffering is good for us, and it passes. Suffering will leave in us the eternal good that God is sending us.

Free yourself from all fear. Let there remain only one fear for a model in you: the fear of God. Let there remain nothing in you from the fear of bears, wolves, diseases and poverty; let in you remain only the fear of God!

In what does the greatness of man reside? In his fairness.

To be strong in life does not just mean to live, but to know in every moment how to act, to know how to use your thoughts, to have the nicest thoughts, and to understand nature and know her laws.

Learn to sing so you can rejuvenate yourself. Music is a way for rejuvenation. Man cannot rejuvenate himself if he does not sing. Music is a science and an art. It is a power. Music is something internal.

You have to know however you treat others that is how God will treat you.

Good and smart is that man who never forgets the Lord in his thoughts.
Good and smart is that man who never forgets the Lord in his feelings.
Good is that one who is always fair to all.

Deposit Love in your head.
Deposit Wisdom in your heart.
Deposit Truth in your actions. In your worldly actions, you must be ruled by the Truth. In your feelings, you must be ruled by Wisdom, and Love to rule the head.

A small job done for God is a great job, but a great job done for you is an insignificant one, a bubble that will pop up. The smallest job done for God after ten years will make you the strongest and most powerful in the world. The smallest job for God is a job that saves. A good day done for God is a lot.

The invisible world wants you to do the smallest good, that good that no one but God can see (a good done in secret). Now that should be your new moral.

The foot of a man cannot step in paradise if he does not think, feel, and act right. God took Adam out of paradise after he broke His law.

Your future life depends on what you do now.

That man who is a pessimist and is looking with darkness on life, do not allow him to put his hand on you. Keep him away even if it is about an insignificant thing.

Love is the meaning of human life.

Those of you who want things to go well must be musical. There must be musicality in your mind, feelings, and actions.

Man must move along the line of the least resistance.

When we talk about Love, we understand the movement of the least resistance. There is no safer road in the world than that of Love. Love is the safest road for a man to walk on.

If you have Love, you have no fear.
If you have fear, you have no Love.

The way to God is the way that always saves you.

You need to study.
You need to thank God.
When you wake up in the morning, thank God.
You have work, thank God.
You have finished your work, thank God.
You go out, thank God.
You do something, thank God.
You come back home, thank God.
You got wet from the rain, thank God.
The wind blew at you, thank God.

The sun shines on you, thank God.
Whatever may happen, thank God.
Somebody looked at you with a bad eye, thank him for it.
You have met an ant, thank God that He has honored you to meet it. Thank God for the clouds. Thank God for the trees and the flowers that have blossomed. In this way, you will accept a good that in no other way can be received. The grateful heart accepts all of God's goods.

The most important thing in the world is Love. The second most important thing is life, and the third is movement and direction.

Think of God constantly. Always think that He thinks about you. If you think differently, you will create an unhappy condition in yourself.

Love, this is the first impulse of Genesis, the first impulse of life. Love is the Divine impulse. It is the nicest thing. It is the first thing that comes in life, the first thing that creates the universe.

We all have to love God. Without Love of God, we will be foreign to one another.

There are teachers now who say, "Pray to the Lord and He will listen to you." If you pray to Him according to all rules of music, He will listen to you, but if you do not, your prayer will remain here on Earth, it won't go to the other world. In other words, your prayer must be sent to God with Love. Without Love, you cannot get the right tune.

Musical Love must take part in the prayer. These things you do not know. You think you can get in paradise without music. No, no. You cannot get in paradise without music. A man who is not musical cannot get in paradise. He can catch a glimpse from the doorstep, but won't be able to cross it.

That which God has put in you (all the gifts, feelings, and abilities that you have) you have to make an effort to develop.

In the world beyond, where you are going to, ignorant people are not wanted. Ignorance does not help anywhere. Studying helps everywhere, in this and the other world.

Bad life cannot bring happiness to man. You must know that bad thoughts, feelings, and actions can never bring something good. In life, one bad deed can serve you as a lesson, but good it can never bring.

If you are seeking good in life, put Love in your head. If you are seeking unhappiness, take the road of lovelessness.

Good is a fruit of Divine Love.

You love good people because they give. They bring God's blessing in the world.

When you see God in people, Love is there. And when people see God in you, Love is there too. That is how it must be understood.

Rule: Talk when you have something nice to say. Do not talk when you have something bad to say.

If you make ten mistakes and you do not rectify them, you become ten times weaker. But if you make ten mistakes and you set them right, you become ten times stronger. That is why you have to set your mistakes right, to become stronger, better, and more reasonable. Every mistake is a stain that must be removed.

You all must be full with good! The good is from God! Reason is from God! And Love is from God! And when we give them away, then we take part in Divine life. Then the physical life on Earth has meaning.

Man must be three things: good, reasonable, and loving.

If you do evil, you always get weaker.
If you refrain from evil, you win.

If you refrain from doing good, you become weaker. But if you do good, you become stronger.

What is that that can put mood in the soul? Thoughts about God. If you start thinking about Him, your mood will change for the better right away.

Why should we be good? I have to be good in myself because on that depends my happiness.

God does not want from us to allow bad thoughts in ourselves, but if we happen to allow them, God wants from us to set them right.

When you wake up in the morning, think of God, for the Love that He has toward you, and then for the Love of Him that you have. **Strive to show Love to whomever it might be, wherever it may be, and whatever the conditions are.**

Every bad thought is staining the face of the Lord, the hands of the Lord, and staining the feet of the Lord. I say: I should not sin. I shall not stain that One Who loves me. And I am telling you: Do not stain that One Who loves you.

To tell people's mistakes is not a science. If the learned man seeks people's mistakes, he will cripple his mind. It is a science to seek the good in man; the good is a science. Because the good is reasonable, it has order.

Happiness is achieved only in freedom. Always in life a man's many desires will divert him from the right way. The man's many desires divert him from achieving the happiness he is seeking.

We have to understand what thing Love is. Love, this is the great good of life.
What thing is Wisdom? Wisdom is the great good of knowledge. Man needs knowledge.

What thing is Truth? Truth is the greatest good for freedom. Without Truth, there is no freedom. Freedom gives man all opportunities to achieve everything he is looking for.

If you study without Love, your success will be problematic and temporary. Whatever work you do in the world, if you do not put the Divine in it, your success will be problematic and temporary too.

All those who love God succeed.
All those who fail, fail in their Love of God.

No man has the right to impose on a woman to marry him. As he is free to make his own choice, so is she to make hers.

Till we worry over the smallest things in the world, it shows that the Divine Love is not in us.

Why is there suffering? Suffering is a refresher. If you have no suffering, twice bigger mishaps will come on you.

Love is that quality that will connect you with God. A greater good than Love you cannot find. And a greater mishap than that to lose Love you cannot get. The greatest mishap for you is to lose Love. When you lose Love, you will find death.

You cannot live in Love and be unhappy.

They say: No one can go to God if he is not pure. No one can go to God if he is not good, merciful, and reasonable.

All tests that we get are to ennoble us. The difficulties and the stumbling blocks that you meet are an educational means. Without suffering and tests, you cannot have any gains.

In "Divine Love," I understand the following: I realize that all beings, whatever they may be, have equal rights for Divine good. That kind of understanding is Divine Love. If you do not understand it like that, it is not Divine Love.

Happiness can be achieved only when we realize that goal that God has put in life—and that goal in man's life is God.

Man, who wants to fulfill the will of God, he must be ready for any work. He must use even the smallest occasions to do it. Let's say a poor man's handkerchief falls from his pocket. You could be a professor, pick it up, and give it to him.

Knowledge is Divine blessing.

Firstly, do not see the bad in the world and do not take upon yourself to reform it. See the bad in yourself firstly, do not critique yourself, but after you find all of your mistakes, take it upon yourself to rectify them. Do not rectify them all at once, but start with a little one each day.

The goal in the world is God only. And all people in the world must have as a goal to achieve the Divine in themselves.

The first thing in Love is to educate the heart.
The first thing in Divine Wisdom is to educate and train the mind.
The first thing in Divine Truth is to educate and train the will. Thus only we can achieve that what we wish for the future.

If we want things to be turned for the good, we have to go by the law of Love. The law of Love is the law of life.

The Love that has touching points on Earth is physical Love.
The Love that you feel like warmth is spiritual Love.
But the Love that you feel like light, that Love is Divine Love.

Man must learn to feel his neighbor's pain. Somebody is hungry. Give him something from yourself. Not doing that is a crime.

Human Love is changeable. Divine Love, however, is the most steadfast; there are no changes in it.

If you let Divine Love in your spirit, you will acquire power; the power is the light that moves.
If Love acts in your soul, it will give you warmth. Warmth is the nicest, it is necessary, because with warmth, everything grows and ripens. Without warmth, man cannot grow and ripen.

There is nothing nicer in man's life than this, to be a pure son of God, with pure thoughts, pure wishes, and pure actions. Not to be just for a day, but from the day you were born till the day you leave Earth, be an excellent son.

Know that if you do not love, you cannot enter the Kingdom of God. No one's foot can ever step in there if he does not love.

If you live with Love in the world, you will have one result; if you live without Love, you will have another. If you live with hope, you will have one result; if you live without hope, you will have another.

If you love your neighbor, you love God. If you love him, that means you serve God. If you do not, it means you do not serve God.

Man, for his own good and in order to become what he wants, he must love God.

The smart, good, and healthy man is a rich man.

The good things that happen to you now are due to the good that you have done in the past. They are coming back to you. And the good that you are doing now will come back to you. Keep that as a law. You all must have the holy feeling to treat others well. Because when you treat them well, that good will come back to you.

Love in which we are not ready to serve, that Love is not the right one.

Love in which we want to command is not right. To blackmail somebody because he loves us is not Love, but coercion. In Love are shown the nicest feelings and thoughts. I want your Love to be absolutely selfless.

You have to know that what you see in others, that is you.

Man must have lofty ideals. The height of your ideals that is what your culture will be. Love is one lofty ideal.

There is nothing more dangerous for a man than this, to fall in love with himself.

Firstly, the mind must be purified. It must be absolutely clean. That is possible. It is possible with the Law of Love.

Love is a power that comes down from God. Love is a clean power.

Reasonable is that one who knows how to act in any given situation.

Know that the smallest lie or the smallest hypocrisy of yours will bring you after some time, maybe after ten, twenty, a hundred, five hundred, or a thousand years, the greatest mishaps that you have ever dreamed of. And the smallest good that you perform, that good after one, two, ten, or ten thousand years, will bring you one of the greatest goods. The smallest good performed has twenty-five years of life.

Lie carries in itself an explosive substance that destroys. Hypocrisy carries in itself an explosive substance that destroys too.

In order for you to be happy, you have to be strong and healthy and to understand nature.

If you know how to talk well, you will be happy. Correct speech.

The Divine world is the one that brings happiness because everything that you want is in that world. The Divine world is the world of all opportunities, a world of bliss and happiness.

An unrealized good deed produces evil.
The rectified evil produces good.

Until suffering becomes pleasant to you, you won't be able to understand Divine Love.

Every day you have to have an improvement in your thoughts, feelings, and actions.

When you leave home, say, "Bye" (or "See you later"); the other family members and the children say, "May God be with you! May the Blessing of God be with you!"

Love is the way of life. Where there is Love, there is light.

Love that cannot free man is not Love.
Wisdom that cannot enlighten man is not Wisdom.
Truth that cannot bring man to Love is not Truth.

If you want to be free, do not see the mistakes in others.

A new epoch is coming. I call it "the epoch of brotherhood and sisterhood, the epoch of entering paradise."

Learn to respect one another. You are all conductors of God's blessing. And if you do not respect somebody, you deprive yourself of Divine blessing. As much as you love people, you will benefit from their good. Whomever you may love, you are the beneficiary of that Love.

A good man is everyone who speaks the Truth.

You all should pray for one another, or think well for one another. When you meet somebody, wish him well.

God lives in everything. His spirit is present even in the smallest being.

You say: "What should we preach to people?" Tell them: Without Love of God, life has no meaning. A sick man comes to you, tell him: Without Love of God, man cannot be healthy. You come to an ignorant man, tell him: Without God, man cannot become learned. You come to a bankrupt merchant, tell him: Without Love of God, trade will not be going well. Tell the people: Without Love of God, life cannot be understood. I say one cannot preach everywhere in the same manner.

The separation from God always produces suffering.

If you do not make sacrifices, you cannot progress in life.

Love carries the strongest vibrations. If you have Love in yourself, you will be able to open your way anywhere. If people lived by the law of Love, if they had that consciousness to live by it, they would still have difficulties, but they would be able to solve them easily.

All the mishaps that we now have happen because of the big Love that we have for ourselves and the lovelessness that we have for our neighbors.

God requires from us to love one another. All people in the world must study this law of Love.

I say if we love God, He will fulfill each and every one of our thoughts, wishes, and deeds; that's why we say we have to study the law of Love without fear, but to tell in our consciousness: "Lord, teach me to live as you want me to live."

The man who does not lose cannot win.
The man who does not suffer cannot have joy.

There are certain sufferings that are Divine, and there are certain sufferings that are human; from those you must keep guard.

Give honor to one another. Respect one another. If you do not give honor, you won't receive honor. God wants that. Everyone who wants to change God's law, for him suffering is coming. Suffering is a reaction, so it can put us in the right way.

Create in yourself right thoughts for people, so you do not stop your evolution. Think about people as God thinks about them. Cooperate in this, that God has meaning, and assist in uplifting people. By doing this, you will elevate yourself too. If all of you live like that, you will uplift yourself.

God is the freest Being. If we do not want to fulfill His Will, we cannot be free. If we pay attention to His thoughts, we will be freest in our thoughts. God is the freest being because He loves all and hates nobody. Sometimes He corrects people because we get in conflict with Him. When He punishes us that means we have gotten into conflict with Him.

The subject of Love is the Truth. Keep in mind that in you true Love cannot be awakened until you love the Truth.

If you do not come to love the Truth, lies definitely will show up; that is unavoidable.

If Divine Love and Divine Wisdom live in me, only then am I a smart, learned, and holy man. Saints in whom there is no Divine Love or Wisdom are not saints. Priests and preachers in whom there is no Divine Love or Wisdom are not priests and preachers.

Truly, there are only two who put stamps on people: Christ and the devil. What is the difference between those two stamps? I will explain to you the difference so I don't leave you in ignorance.
The qualities of the Christ stamp, the stamp of Love, are Love, joy, peace, long patience, meekness, humbleness, kindness, compassion, faith, and abstention. The stamp of the devil is 666 and his qualities are adultery, sorcery, jealousy, blasphemy, and so forth. If you see in somebody the stamp of Christ, give him a brotherly hand. If you see on someone's forehead the stamp of the antichrist, the devil, go around him.

There is no other power except the Love that could save you. That power is positive and absolute. If somebody says that he can be saved through some other power, he does not understand Divine Truths. The Lord needs people who can carry His Love. When I talk to you about Love, you imagine the love that you have for your children, brothers, sisters, and so forth. No, uplift yourself one step higher than that love that you have. To love your daughter is natural, to love your son, sister, or brother is natural, but to love your enemy, that is heroic.

How to love our enemy? I will explain so we can understand each other. The law is this: Someone did you the greatest evil or the greatest mischief in the world, and one day the Lord takes away everything from him, and as the poorest beggar, sends him to your home. If you accept him most kindly, feed him, give him water, and do not remind him anything about the evil he did to you in the past, and do not threaten him, that means you love your enemy. You will ask me: "How to love our enemy? Only when the Lord takes out the nails and the teeth of the wolf, and until he has reformed, I do not recommend you caress him or accept him in your home.

You must be natural; your soul must breathe Love. When you enter somebody's home, you must bring blessing and joy for everyone in it. If there is a sick person in the house, roll up your sleeves and do the laundry, set it in order, and clean up their house. If those people have no financial means, bring them some flour or something else. You may ask, "Shall I do this every day?" You do that today, because you are appointed for a duty, and do not think about tomorrow. Tomorrow somebody else will be appointed for a duty and will come and do that.

This teaching is connected with that Great Being in the world who we call God and Who is shown in our souls under the symbols of Love and Wisdom. We all have that Love and Wisdom. Our understanding of the spiritual world, our communication with the other world, depends on how those two powers are shown in us. No one can be a psychic or some public figure, reformer, mother or father if those two powers do not live in his mind and heart. There are no two opinions on that. If you want to be strong and firm and to know the meaning of life, arm yourself with those two powers and you will see the reform that will happen with you. Make a small reform in yourself, but let it be absolute, there should be no two thoughts in you to hesitate whether it is like that or not. You will say, "This is a hard job." This is not a hard thing to do; it is ten times easier than what you do. You do a lot of hard work, but the teaching of Love and Wisdom is not a hard one.

Heaven and Earth will pass away, but God's Law of Love and Wisdom inevitably will be applied

Heroic is this, to love me when I insult you, not when I give you gifts.
Sometimes an insult is worth more than a kiss.
Sometimes it happens somebody passes out and in order to awaken him, people slap him on the face.

Apply Love in your heart and Wisdom in your mind, free yourself from all those old beliefs and delusions, free yourself from the past, and begin to work on your new virtues. Be heroes to show sincerely all of your thoughts and actions. I don't want you to just say you have decided to be sincere, good, etc., but to actually act that way.

Man must free himself from everything obscene. It must completely disappear from him; there should not remain any remembrance of it in him.

The man of the new culture must equally be glad when he gets newborns and when they die or depart for the other world. This is heroic!

Until we decide to make a living exclusively through work, till then the blessing of God won't come. I would rather visit a house regardless of how poor it is, knowing that everything in it is earned with honest work, than to go to a rich house where everything is made on the backs and tears of others. If we all give up dishonest inheritances, we will set the world right soon. You will say, "Let's use that stolen money for the Lord!" The Lord does not need stolen houses, stolen money. The only thing that the Lord needs is people with noble thoughts and noble hearts who are ready to sacrifice themselves. When I talk about self-sacrifice, I am not referring to its ordinary meaning, but to sacrificing yourself in the great law of Love, to denying yourself everything impure, and to connecting with that One Who works in the name of loftiness.

One saint who lived in the desert for twenty years worked hard on himself so he could afterward become strong and work for the people. One day while walking and reasoning, he saw a pot full of gold buried by somebody, but now opened from torrential rains. When he saw it, he jumped right away and ran away from it. His comrade, who was working with him, got interested in knowing why the saint was running. He saw the money and said to himself: "Amazing, running from money." He took the money, made churches, hospitals, and schools. He became proud of what he did and one day he asked the Lord: "Lord, tell me, are you pleased with my deeds?" The Lord sent him an angel who told him: "All your goods done with the found money put on a scale do not weigh as much as the jump of your brother."

The human heart must not get attached to wealth. Man must become rich, but by mind and heart. The riches in the world are an expression of human virtues.

The noblest people in the world are those who have suffered the most; those who have not suffered a lot are not noble. The most learned people are those who have studied the most. People who have not studied a lot remain simple. It is amazing when people in the world want to become smart, learned, and strong, but without working. They want the spirit to come in them, but how? They want to get a magic wand and with it *allez* pass by! And then they will state: "Now I will set Bulgaria right real soon if they only give her to me. And so on. How will they set Bulgaria right? They'll put gallows everywhere and if you are guilty of something, to the gallows. But is that a genius thing?"

There is only one reasonable sower in the world and He is God. There is only one principle in the world, and it penetrates the whole space, all human souls, and it is not in a specific form or in a man, but it is everywhere and He is God.

The new teaching requires from you to be heroes, to be barefoot, but to walk in life honestly and justly. I would rather walk barefoot than skin an ox; I would rather go hungry than to take the life of a hen that does not want to sacrifice herself for me, and with it to cause her suffering. This kind of action means there are great deeds in us; this means the Sower of the new seed to come in us.

When God is in you, you can do anything, but without Him you can do nothing. When God is in you, you will be soaked with great ideas and you will never be discouraged.

And so, let there be absolutely no cheating, lie, and doubt among you.

Knowledge accompanied by Love ennobles.

Pusillanimous people are those who use the lie. The weak in character like to lie. Weak people cannot fulfill their duties; weak people cannot keep their word.

One must be faithful to himself in all things he does. When somebody believes in one thing, but does another, he commits a great crime.

For a man to get elevated, he needs to be put to the test. His honesty must be tested, and if he does not steal and lie, he is an honest man. Tell me if we look for someone who never lied in his life, will we find one? I say if we find only one honest man in Bulgaria, she will be the greatest country, and that man will be like a precious stone where there is none like it. That man or woman will be the most precious thing.

There is no greater sin than killing. That man who dares to kill somebody he is a demonic one, his father is the devil. For killing, there is no forgiveness. This is written in the Divine book. For killing, there is only punishment in the world. Absolutely no killing is allowed!

Because it is said that man is made in the image and likeness of God, when you kill a man, with that you have destroyed the Divine. When you kill a man, when you kill the most lofty and noble in man, with it, you have committed the greatest crime.

Every teacher, every mother, and every father must write thus: "Absolutely no killing is allowed!" That is because we are all connected with one another with karma. One committed killing is bared by all.

Your husband or wife is raising a quarrel, say: "Love and agreement!" And he or she will soften.

Now somebody asks, "What are morals?" The first moral of the Divine teaching of Love is absolutely no killing is allowed!

Everyone should love his brother, but not only that, he should go further to love his enemy. This Christ applied when he was on the cross, he prayed for them, saying: "God forgive them, for they know not what they do." Only this can be real philosophy.

Everyone must stand up against violence and say that which is going on in the world is not in accordance with the Christ teaching, is not in accordance with God's Love.

Why did Christ come on Earth, what was His basic idea? The idea of Love, which can solve all issues (mental, emotional, and social), is the law of the living Love. In what specifically rests this living Love? To know that every man in the world feels and suffers like you do and has such needs as you have. Consequently, to enter fully in his situation and to be ready to help him as you would do for yourself. This is a philosophy, this is a science, which will be applied in the future.

Fear is the greatest disease that modern people have. It is a trap; it is a weakness of the human character, and ninety-nine percent of all crimes are due to fear. Consequently, every one of you who wants to be a hero, he must have absolutely no fear in his heart. His heart must be full of Love.

Everyone who wants to be beautiful like an angel must develop in himself the feeling of brotherhood and sisterhood. This is a law.

I want you now all of you to become brothers and sisters, but you have to be sincere, to speak that what is in your hearts.

If you do not love the Lord with all of your heart, soul, mind, and strength, where are you going to take Love from? Love is not taken from the market.

No one should criticize anyone. No one should criticize his brother.

Man is young till he loves. If he stops loving, he is old. If he loves, he is healthy. If he stops loving, he is sick. If he loves, he is learned. If he stops loving, the knowledge disappears. This is how it is; everyone can check it out for himself.

You are applying the present teaching like this: "Lord, let it be your will, but ours to be done! Lord, let it be your Love, but ours to be done!" I would say, "Lord, to be our will, but yours to be done! Lord, to be our love, but Yours to be done!"

These are the maxims that man can apply: Man who has love there is no power that can oppose him. He will have new understanding; there would be no mishaps in his home, but peace.

The character of man strengthens with the fulfillment of any idea, but weakens when he postpones its fulfillment. And so, not fulfilling the ideas caries reverse hits on man's character.

What you will be born in the future depends on your present life, because the geniuses, the great people, who show up in the world are not chicks that hatch now. Some say, "How I wish to be a genius, to be a great man!" Yes, but you had to work in the past on all of your lofty thoughts, to realize them, to fulfill them.

Any man through work and persistence can overcome all difficulties that show up in his life.

Only in reasonable life there is life; only between reasonable beings can Love be manifested. There is no love in unreasonable life.

In how many ways can man be saved? He can be saved in one way only and that is the way of Love. We save people through Love. Then I tell to all of you: "Love the Lord with all your heart, with all your mind, and with all your strength, and you, your home, your nation, and the whole of humanity will be saved. Love the Lord and run that Love through all of your essence. Then not only will you be saved, but you will become heir of the Kingdom of God.

You ask, "Will I enter the kingdom of God?" Look, if Love has entered your heart, soul, and mind, you will enter the kingdom of God. You also ask, "Will I resurrect?" Look, if you have Love in your heart, soul, and mind, and strength, you will resurrect, but if you do not, whatever they tell you is a lie. That is how the great Truth from life's point of view rests.

Those of you in whom the higher consciousness is awakened and want to live as reasonable beings, let start working with Love, let them inflect the noun love, and conjugate the verb love (I love, you love, he loves, she loves, etc.). When you do this exercise, look at the people around you, whether they become better or worse. But in this law, there are some exceptions, which consist of the following: When you start working with those words at the beginning, you will notice an improvement, then worsening, then greater improvement, which will change to greater worsening, again improvement, but greater, again improvement, but greater, again worsening, and after a series of crises, you will come to a healthy condition.

ONLY LOVE WILL SAVE YOU.

Be brave and decisive and speak only the Truth.

Truth is a condition of the human soul, which is in absolute calm and in harmony with the source of life.

The only one who can lead you to vice is you. When you get into vice by yourself, then anyone from outside can get you into vice, too. Somebody says, "They led me into temptation." No, you fell into temptation by yourself.

Real is this that we have for a given moment in our consciousness. There, in the consciousness, lies true happiness.

Do not expect your happiness from anywhere outside yourself. The one who is awakened must expect the happiness from himself. If you are healthy, if you have a good mind, sound will, and pure heart, you are happy.

And so, the actual, the real, is that higher Love that has nothing in common with your present feelings and disposition. That higher Love is known by that when it touches a fool, he becomes a smart and wise man; when it touches a dead man, he resurrects and comes to life; when it touches a man with leprosy, the leprosy immediately disappears; and when it touches a wounded, discouraged heart, it immediately resurrects. It performs wonders. It is great, mighty, and whatever it touches, it gets created and built. This science for the great Love is worth studying. All knowledge of contemporary science from eight thousand years ago to the present put together in its result, in its effect, are not worth even a single waving of this great Love.

Consequently, there is what to be studied, and I am telling you that from now on you have a lot to study. You are already awakened. Be brave and do not give in to any doubts from anywhere. No matter what others tell you, be faithful to your heart, mind, and will, be faithful to your spirit and soul. This is the first principle. If you are faithful to yourself, you will be faithful to all; if you are not faithful to yourself, you cannot be faithful to anyone.

Turn to God. Believe in that Love that arranges everything at once.

If you acquire reasonable life in the world, you have acquired Love, but if you enter unreasonable life, you will have torment.

Evil increases evil. Good increases good. These are laws that act in the world.

Doubt is an infirmity of man's mind, hatred and envy of man's heart.

Say, "My heart is warm, my soul is fresh, my mind is bright, and my spirit is robust." Why? Because I live in the Law of Love, in which there are no changes. Now do you know how much this understanding that I gave you is worth? It is worth $25 billion. There are people who have taken 20 to 25 existences (lives) to learn this formula. You will say, "It is a very simple thing; we know these things." But you never knew these things by the way they are experienced—warm, fresh, bright, robust. Now, when you go home, I want you to apply this understanding to yourself.

We have not come on Earth as guests. Earth is a great school in which we have come to study.

Have you had a conversation with your soul? How can you do this? This is the greatest question. Talk to your soul, and you will understand a lot of great things. If you do not, you will be a first-class fool. Soul, this is the mother of man. Man has two mothers in the world. One is Maya, this who covers man in matter. This mother has given man all the misleading. There is another mother who is called the Divine soul, and that the Indians call Nirvana. When you enter Nirvana, you forget about all of your mishaps, and you are ready to bear your sins as well the sins of all. When Christ says, "If you do not deny yourself from your mother," under the word "mother" He understands mother as Maya, who tells you: "I gave you a birth, you will listen to me, and you will have morals, but look to provide for yourself in life. You are allowed to commit one crime for your good."

What does it mean to find the Lord? To find the Lord means the great law of Love to start working in you.

Christ's writing on the ground.
When the adulteress was brought before Christ, he wrote on the ground: "You are far away from understanding the Divine ways; you are far away from judging."

Love with money is not bought and not sold. Remember these things. Wisdom with money is not bought and with money is not sold. Justice with money is not bought and with money is not sold. Virtue with money is not bought and with money is not sold.

The toughest people are the egoists. When a tough man climbs to rule the world, he will produce the greatest mishaps.

No form, no organization, can make you happy, but they can serve you as a condition to grow and strengthen.

If you ask me how the existence of Divine Love is proven, I will tell you that it is proven by this, that evil exists. Because God loves you, He has given you limitless rights, but you will bear the consequences of your actions. Thus, if you are asked by what is Love known, you will answer, "Love is known by this, that it allows evil." But why are people discontent and evil? Because Love is not inside of them, but outside.

I am teaching you the true art of life. I don't tell anybody "believe," but "try it." These laws are not mine, they exist from limitless eternity, they have always existed, and life rests upon them. I have told them and many others will tell them that Truth and Love are not a monopoly, they are principles for all of us, and all can benefit from them.

My wish for you is not to be happy, but be with pure hearts, and to strengthen in Wisdom and knowledge. If I come in your home and find happiness as an ideal, I will tell you: Take down this icon from here, and put something else in its place. When you go home, take down the icon of happiness and put in its place the following inscription: "Love requires feat, bravery, and decisiveness in life for uplifting all our brothers and sisters in this world." Put this inscription in and look what reform will happen. Put it in and apply it. When you take down that false divinity and put the new inscription up, you will hear the angels from above singing and all the blessing will come upon you. These are not philosophical claims, this is not hypnotizing, this is not casting a spell (bewitching), this is a great philosophy in life, which will make you with robust spirits, bright minds, and pure hearts, it will make you citizens of that kingdom that is entering the cosmos of the universe.

Man's richness is in his brain.

In the Divine world, every form is an emblem of a definite and known content, an emblem of definite and known life. So in whatever form you create for yourself on Earth, when you enter with it in the other world, on it they will read not just how you lived on Earth, but in thousands of other previous lives, and they will know all details of your life, everything that you have done with the greatest secrets. Everything will be open, which is why the Scripture says, "There is nothing hidden that will not be revealed. There is nothing kept secret that will not come to light."

Every woman who has removed her baby (through a doctor, an abortion, or by other means) will bear her curse for four generations. Yes, you can bite your lips; you can bite them four times. Nature knows only one way of taking out a baby. She says, "You will take it out only on the ninth month, the ninth minute, and the ninth second."

Every unfulfilled promise leaves on man's face a line with no form and he becomes rude, rude till he turns to a mooncalf. Never try to destroy a Divine thought in you even if it costs you your life. Step up for that nice form, step up for its content, step up for that idea. This form, this content, this idea will resurrect you anew, but if you lose that form, you lose everything. Then the man who lost his human form comes on Earth not like a human, but in a lower form. If he happens to lose that one too, he will begin to degrade.

Every single hair is full of energy, magnetism, and electricity. Some ask me why I leave my hair long. I have long hair for the following simple reason: Whoever wants to be healthy must always have long hair, because it retains more of the electrical and magnetic energy. With the hair cut, man deprives himself of that energy. I do not like hair cutting. Hair must be left as long as to the bottom of the ears. Whoever breaks this rule and cuts his hair above the top part of his ears will be paying for his sins. And so nature has put for cultured people the following rule: Men should not cut their hair below the top part of their ears, and women are allowed to have long hair, though they can cut it. Everything that we support has its meaning. The hair brings health and keeps the head warm as well.

The Divine life does not rest in fasting, does not rest in torturing the body in the distortion of our minds and our bodies. The Divine life does not rest in all of this that now exists. It, the Divine life, is a great harmony. Eat, but not too much, do not overeat; sleep, but not too much; dress nicely, but nothing extraordinary. Have what is useful, but necessary. And thus all of you must live.

If you talk about this what you love, you tarnish it. When you love, be silent.

Be brave and decisive in life, know that the world is created for you to study, but not to create bad thoughts and to distort your life.

The qualities of the new man are justice, holiness, and Truth. Justice is for the heart, the feelings, and the soul; Truth is for the mind and the spirit, but holiness this is the inner connection between the heart and the mind. Consequently, if justice does not lie in your heart as a foundation, and Truth has not moved in your mind and in your thoughts, and holiness does not create a connection, a place for a union between the heart and the mind, I ask you then how will you understand the Christ teaching? It is not understandable without these qualities, and all who try it say it is not a feasible teaching.

All people who have stomach ailments must know that the Truth is not in their minds. This is exactly defined, without any exceptions. You say, "My stomach is upset." The Truth is not in your mind. What should we do? You will bring the Truth in your mind, and you will see that your stomach will be OK.

Justice must lie down in man's heart or soul; say it as you like. When justice lies down in man's heart, in man's soul, he will have a healthy heart, a healthy breathing system, no palpitation. Every valve disease, every lung disease, is due to the lack of justice. Consequently, if you ask me why we need justice in the world, as we suffer from injustice, I will tell you: Justice is needed to keep our hearts and lungs in harmony because the heart is needed for setting the lungs right. If you have no justice, your heart and lungs will be exposed to distortion, and when that happens, you will be pressed by melancholy, which contemporary people go through. If you ask me why you are melancholic, I will tell you because justice is not lying down deep in your life.

Now people lack something essential. The Truth is not in their minds, justice is not in their hearts, and holiness does not connect those things. Now I do not say this applies for everyone, there are exceptions; I call these exceptions "holy exceptions."

Only with the qualities of Justice and Truth can man understand the new teaching.

If things in the world do not go well for you and if you are not happy and if your life is messed up, all that is due to the lack in you of justice, Truth, and holiness.

And so if you do not put in the qualities of justice, Truth, and holiness as their connection in you, you will go bankrupt; this applies to everyone. If you hesitate to do this, in the end you will live through the most terrible suffering. For all those who do not abide by this great law of justice, Truth, and holiness, the greatest suffering is coming. And when the suffering comes, know that it is due to that, that justice is not in your heart and Truth is not in your mind. To be free of suffering, apply this precept of mine. Don't just say, "I believe, I love God." You cannot love until you have justice in your heart; you cannot think until you have Truth in your mind, and you cannot do something holy until you have holiness in yourself as a connecting thread.

Only to such a will is every action submitted. When Christ said, "If you have faith like a grain of mustard seed, you can say to this mountain, 'Move from here to there,' and it will move." He talked about that man in whom justice, Truth, and holiness live. Do not fall into the illusion that you can go without these qualities.

Each nation must have in its heart justice, in its mind Truth, and its will to be strengthened with holiness. So is this true for each home, each society, each church, and each school, without any exceptions. Then we will have a great culture.

And so if your mind is suffering, put the Truth in it, if your heart is suffering, put justice in it, and if your will is not strong, put holiness in it. This is a means to strengthen yourself and to live. What comes out from that one in whom there is no justice, Truth, or holiness? If you do not have justice, Truth, and holiness, Love cannot show up.

Only then when justice enters into your heart and Truth enters into your mind, only then can we be one with Christ and can we say that we are one with Christ. And then whatever we ask for will be given to us.

You will say, "Let's work for justice and Truth next year." This will never happen if you keep postponing. This Lord who has sent you on Earth has written on the door through which the spirits come down to Earth this: "Everyone who comes down on Earth, to study, to finish his education, is obliged to put justice in his heart, Truth in his mind, and holiness in his will, and that one who does not do it will never be allowed to pass through that door." That is how it is written. I have read that inscription on the door, and if you do not believe it, go and check it out. Ask your saints and let them refute my assertion whether it is or not written on that door. But there is also another door, a second door, through which you have passed, and on it is written: "Do not deal with Truth, it is an empty thing; do not deal too much with justice, and you can live without holiness too. If you want to live, you do not need justice, Truth, and holiness." So, you have mixed those two inscriptions and are saying: "With justice, Truth, and holiness, one cannot live. Everyone cannot be just, truthful, and holy." No, everyone can be just and must be just; everyone can speak the Truth; everyone can love the Truth and live with the Truth. This is the essential teaching, it is with cardinal importance for each one of you personally, and when you apply it on Earth, you will solve all issues that you are dealing with the way they should be. Consequently, you all have to step up for these three principles. If you do not put justice in your heart, Truth in your mind, and holiness in your will, nothing will come. If you wait for your priest first to become holy and you afterward, nothing will come.

You say, "When will Christ come?" If justice does not enter into your heart, Truth into your mind, and holiness into your will, Christ will never come. But if you put justice in your heart, Truth in your mind, and holiness in your will, Christ will come right away.

And so, if you are asked, "What is the fundamental distinction of our teaching from others?" you will tell them, "Our teaching says this: 'Let's dress up in the image of God, in the image of the new man, created in justice, Truth, and holiness.'" And if you are asked, "Where are justice, Truth, and holiness?" You will tell them that justice must lie down in our hearts, Truth in our minds, and holiness in our will, in our strength, in our body, and everywhere our lives must be in harmony. This is the new practical application of our teaching.

If you have these three elements (justice, Truth, and holiness), Christ will come in you, you will be one with Christ, and you will be able to say, "Christ and I are one."

In man, made in the image and likeness of God, means: man is made in the mind and the spirit of God. We are made in His spirit and thought.

God in His essence is unchangeable.

There is a rule in Love: When you love somebody, you equalize him with yourself; you will give him qualities, as you give to yourself, as he is equal to you.

If you do not give freedom to others, you do not love them.

Love is something spontaneous. The spontaneous things are Divine. It is a great Divine law that gives an impulse. And all things are due to that Divine, to that Divine impulse. If you in a given moment resist that Divine impulse, you will create a mishap for yourself. You can be as useful to others as much as you are responsive to this Divine impulse that is in you.

Christ did not apply anything by force. He said, "If you love me, you will keep my commandments."

Every time when we commit a certain crime, God moves away from us, but when we do a good deed, He is always present in us.

Do not keep your sins in your consciousness because you will tarnish yourself. If possible, keep the sins one kilometer away from yourself.

Man should never allow a bad word on his tongue, because people will be held accountable for each empty word they say.

The greatest mishap for you is to be deprived from the right to be reincarnated, that is, to be banned from coming on Earth. This the church calls "to be eternally locked up."

You may have a hundred children, but what are the use and benefit of them if you have not taught them the Divine law? What is the benefit of such children if Love, the great stimulus, is not planted in them? Faith and hope are from Love, but without the first inner awakening in you, no faith or hope can be conceived.

Law: Love only conceives Love in people, hatred cannot conceive Love. Hatred can coerce one to love out of fear, but afterward fear conceives twice as much hatred as before. Fear is not a quality of Love, but of evil, of sins that we have committed in the past. Fear is the unknown. All evil and wicked people are very fearful.

Outside of Love, all things are dead, unconscious, that is, they have only a mechanical movement.

Christ says, those who have no love do not know the Father, because God is Love. And so lay down the thought: Outside of Love, life does not exist.

To think about God means to think about the greatest, there is nothing more valuable than it (the greatest).

Man who cannot sacrifice himself he does not know God. This is the great teaching that Christ has preached.

In Love, there is no fear or doubt, and this is a great, great law. The people of love should have no fear; whoever has fear for him there is no love, there is no knowledge of Christ.

Everyone who is afraid of death and of the devil, he does not know God. God has put the devils in their places to urge the people to work because they are lazy.

To love a friend is one thing; to love an enemy, it is a different thing. If you hate your enemy, you will become like him, you will get down to his level. You will say, "To help my enemy." Your enemy never should be paid back with hatred, but with Love. Whoever pays back with evil, he will follow the evolution of the sinful spirits.

So what of that, that your brother is sinful? Help him, clean him up, give him clothes, and dress him up. "But you are sinful; go away, I do not want to help you." This is not the Divine Christian teaching.

Under man's salvation, I understand to enter in life's conditions to restore that prime connection between man and God. Every being that loses his relations with the prime connection needs salvation. No other salvation outside of this exists. That is how I understand salvation, and that is how the Lord understands it. Christ, and the saints, and thus all righteous people, will understand it, but all fools will understand it in a different way.

To the young man who asked Christ what to do to inherit an eternal life, Christ replied, "Do not kill!" Killing is one of the causes of breaking these connections with God; be careful not to break the connections with the body, the connections between your brothers. "Do not lie." Lying is the second cause of breaking the connections with salvation. "Do not steal and do not be a false witness." They also break the connection with salvation. "Honor your father and mother and your neighbors." The first five commandments are the Christ teaching, but the second five, the Moses law. The first five commandments belong to the present epoch; they are the law of the spirit, but the other five are the laws of the physical world. Christ explained the reasons that break up the connections and the reasons that connect, and he said, "Honor your father, your mother, and your neighbors, and you will be saved."

In the commandment "Do not kill," the word "kill" has a wide meaning and application. You will say to yourself: "Glory to God, I have not killed anybody." There is not even a single man among you who can brag he never killed. I can prove that to you with data, but let's leave this issue on the side. "Killing" infers not only when you kill somebody, but also when you kill in yourself a good thought or a good wish. Killing is also when you kill a good thought in somebody.

Christ says, "Do not kill." This means in your wishes there should be no thought of destruction of any good wishes or any good thoughts that God has put in, but on the contrary you must cultivate them. If you kill all of that (the good wishes and thoughts), your life will become meaningless.

Every wish in man to do a good to somebody is preceded by another thought, from the law of Love. Only when in you arises a wish of compassion and Love, then only will you be ready to do a good deed. There is no man who can do a good deed without a good thought.

A thought that can change your life is stronger than any physical being. Every good thought brings something, but does not take.

The sin in us emerges from not allowing God to manifest Himself. We stop God in His good thoughts and wishes that act in us.

The only things that can change the heart of a sinner are hunger and suffering when they reach their extreme limits.

"Do not kill, do not lie, do not be a false witness." This is the law of reincarnation. And when it is finished, then comes the law of inoculation. The other commandments are "Honor your father and mother, love you neighbor, and give away your possessions." These are the seven commandments that you must keep, and then will come the break and you will become immortal. This is the great salvation, to unite with God, and then you will have thousands times greater goods than the ones you have now.

Always tell one another the truth. If you cannot tell the truth, better keep quiet.

I do not know of other beings as holy, as kind, and as pure as the Lord. I have tried Him millions and millions of times, and He has always been unchangeable in Himself, He has always been kind, but if you sin a lot and do not turn to Him, He will let you bear the consequences of your sins, so you can see for yourself what it means to live without God. It is a great suffering in the world to live without God. There is no need to tell you: Go to God, He is your Father. And you yourself have to turn to Him. If you want your sons and daughters to honor you, put this thought in you to be always with God and see within a year how your life will change.

I love the sinners, the lazy and the good-for-nothing people. I wish that you had the same soft spot toward the sinners, and then the whole world would have had a different look. And Christ had such a soft spot for the sinners and that's why He let Himself be mocked and profaned.

If you do not serve God, you cannot ennoble yourself.

Suffering on Earth is hidden happiness (as in "no pain, no gain.") It is better to suffer for an idea than not to have one. It is better to have some idea, even if you have to go through suffering to have it, than not to have one.

A man who brings good and peace and elevates people is worth more than a whole nation that brings in sorrow, suffering, and destruction for humanity. I am asking, Where was the great Roman Empire when Christ was born? What is left from her? Nothing. There was at that time a man who died as a bandit, but His ideas still exist and reign over the world. He is worth more than the whole Roman Empire. That great man was Christ.

Our Love must be unselfish.

The Word of God is a much higher substance, it is a spiritual matter, from which can be extracted that which is necessary for our lives, but from the lower matter that corrupts our lives, this cannot be done.

Christ has said, "Man can feed himself with every word that comes out of God." Christ proved this. He took five loafs of bread and five fishes, and that is how five thousand people got fed.

I do not have the right to speak that what is not according to the Christ teaching. I have to speak only that what is truth, which is Divine, because for every teaching I will give an answer before God.

Do not think that in the spiritual science things go very quickly. No, they go very slow. The Divine goes from the little to the big, but the human begins with the grand and ends up with the little.

Your faith must be positive, to act inside your mind.

There is no death, but undressing.

As you clean up your houses so you must clean your minds and your hearts. Do not let in your mind bad thoughts. For example, some woman let in herself the thought that her husband goes after other women. Do not let in such a thought, but talk to your husband. Throw out that thought; it does not bring joy. This Divine spirit that lives in us wants to bring us closer, to love one another reasonably, not to do evil.

If you tell your son, "You will be good son," he will really become good. When the mother conceives, she must say, "I believe, I believe, that I will give birth to a good child, I am glad that it will be a good child," and so forth.

Matthew 7:21
"Not everyone who says to me, 'Lord, Lord,' shall enter the kingdom of heaven, but only he who does the will of my Father who is in heaven." Those people who break the will of God do not have His blessing.

Christ says, "In order not to get lost you have to fulfill the Will of your Father!"
In what is concluded the will of This Father? This will is expressed in the form of a law. The first law is: Whatever you do not want to be done to you, do not do that to others.

To tell a lie means to live in the world of disorder; to speak the truth means to live with the reasonable Divine will.

If your things in the world do not go well, start singing and they will go better.

All happiness and mishaps are due to our past actions. If we want to change our future lives we have to understand the fundamental laws that regulate the human will, strength, feelings, and the human consciousness.

When we begin to think about the meaning of the inner life, before all we have to know, that as thinking beings we belong to God, then to humanity, to our nation, to our home, and lastly to ourselves. So, when somebody asks me, "Are you Bulgarian?" I reply, "I am a thinking being who first belongs to God, then to humanity, my nation, my home, and lastly to myself."

The good man's heart must be filled with the nicest wishes, his mind, with the nicest thoughts, but his will, with the nicest actions. Then he will be the highest being.

You say, "I love this man." I know what you love in him. You love his money, his deposit box, his knowledge, teaching, looks and so on. But when he loses his wealth, your love for him disappears. We have to find in man the real man, who is like a Divine ray which came out of God first. That man is our brother.

And so if you love a man for his money, beauty, and knowledge, leave that man, but seek the real one. Christ came to give up His life, not for the rich, but for the poor and the suffering people.

This teaching has application in the education and upbringing of our children. Make an experiment. You have a stubborn; self-willed child that does not honor you, but you want respect from this child. Strive to obliterate all of the negative traits that you have, and begin to think that your child is good and begin to love them.

When a man does not say the very truth, he has said a lie. When one man can not talk with the language of Wisdom, he is foolish. When a man does not act according to the language of Justice and Fairness, he is a bad, evil man.

Man is in the likeness of God, by substance the human soul and spirit have the same thing which the Divine Spirit has. This we can all realize. Somebody says, "I can not do it." - You can, because everything is put into your soul.

Everyone must say, "God has put into me everything; that is why I will do everything He wants."

The Lord has made all of us from one and the same essence; all souls are from one and the same source.

In the word "fool" I do not understand an unreasonable man, but a man who does not have conditions to develop himself. Take one smart man; lock him up in a dark room to stay there for 10 years without opportunities to develop himself, and he will become an idiot. Take the most foolish man and put him in the best conditions, and in 10 years he will improve.

If one teaching elevates you and makes you smarter with more reasoning, then this teaching is Divine; it is a true one.

In the reasonable man I understand a man who has a strong will, strong heart, and strong mind.

Sufferings are a reversal process of rectification so that the evil in us can be turned into good.

Firstly, learn to be patient. There are two types of patience: misery, and forbearance. Misery is imposed upon you, but patience is due to the human will. We should never impose upon people by telling them, "You will believe as I believe." Leave that man to plant his garden as he wants. Do not make plans for him, just give him the seeds.

Believing understands light, but disbelieving - darkness. That's why good is done in light, but evil - in darkness.

Believe that you are a good man. When you get up in the morning tell yourself, "I am a good and smart man because the Lord made me."

John 15:10
"If you keep my commandments, you will abide in my love, just as I have kept my Father's commandments and abide in his love." The word "keep" relates to the human will. To keep the commandments means to fulfill them, which we can do only through our will. Consequently if man does not fulfill the commandments, he cannot abide in Love.

A man who wants to live well with his wife must not define any rules, but must let her be free. Let two men make an experiment: one of them writes laws which his wife must follow, but the other one lets his wife be free. Which family's life will be better? In that one in which the wife goes by her own laws, life will be better, not in the one in which the laws are imposed upon her by her husband (or from outside).

We must know that Christ always comes with the words, "I can," If you say, "I can," Christ is with you. If you say, "I can not, the devil is with you. If you say, "I can live a good Christian life," Christ is with you. If you say, "I can not do this," the devil is with you. You will say, "I am a sinner." Do not say that! The sin is in the human will only; straighten out your will and you will cleanse yourself. Why did the Lord create so much water? - Water is Life, so say, "I made a mistake, but I can clean it up; I can cleanse myself."

Truth always defines the relations that exist. The Truth is in itself concrete. When you have the Truth in yourself, you will feel one inner light in your heart and mind; you will be sure in your convictions and beliefs, and they will be for you one inner power and you will have no fear in your soul. Everyone who is not sure in the truth will hesitate. Consequently, the hesitation in us is a sign that we do not have this absolute truth, because the truth as a concept exists, and in itself is alive.

When we say, "The Head of Your word is Truth," and "God is Truth," we understand one living reality. Consequently, in the physical realm, he who has truth in himself will be one of the smartest, happiest, healthiest, and strongest of people. Those who want to be beautiful -- let them find the truth and all will love them.

Man in whom there is truth is strong; he is immortal and a master of the situation. The whole of nature greets him, and wherever he goes everything, the flowers, animals, rivers, and mountains, greets him. If man does not have truth in himself, the greetings will be reversed.

When you go through the world and people attack you, one of these two is true: either there is no truth in you, or there is no truth in that society. Upon this issue, one must look philosophically.

We love the man when he does good for us. But if he does something evil or mischievous, we all deny him. This is not Divine. It is heroic is love the bad, ugly man. We have to, not just individually, but collectively, create this impulse to love the bad and the ugly.

The only wealth in the world is Love. The only wealth in the world is Wisdom. The only wealth in the world is Truth. These are three things that man must possess. Whoever has them is a truly rich man: Love for the soul, Wisdom for the mind, and Truth for power. Truth is that which brings power and freedom.

If you do not love, your heart will atrophy. Man must love because the heart supports its life through love. And the mind, through thinking, supports its life.

Immortality rests in this: make God master in yourself! Happiness rests in this: do not make yourself a master. Make the Lord the master in yourself. Say, "Whatever you say, Lord, I will fulfill. I will be the servant, and you the Master." If this philosophy does not enter you, <u>one and the same result is expecting the whole world.</u>

The only Mother and the only Father in the world is God. One is your Father! One is the Spirit! In all of you is One and the same! God who talks in me, in you also talks the same. God cannot talk to me that Love is one thing, but to you that Love is something else.

In God there are no weaknesses.

God will turn everything bad into good.

If you are asked, "What are you studying?" reply, "We rejoice in all people because God lives in them." God is inside the world. Since God is inside the world, He will make everything for the good. And this is the Glory of God, that He will turn everything into good.

Some have asked me, "How should our approach toward people be? How should one treat himself? There is only one way: You treat yourself such that you do not lower your dignity. Primarily do not humiliate yourself. If you speak untruthful things, if you do not feel, do not think, and do not act as you are supposed to, you are humiliating yourself. First and foremost, do not humiliate yourself by any means. As God has created you, in that way you will act. This is a difficult job, but all difficult things are achievable. There is no difficult job in the world that cannot be achieved.

Put in your mind and support the following idea: God has created everything in the world for the good.

The brighter the thought becomes in man's mind, and the warmer his feelings become and bring life - the more God is manifested in him. God is manifested through our thoughts and through our hearts.

The true love is known when contradictions come. If you cannot love a man with the contradictions that you encounter, what love do you have? Imagine that a very smart man is fixing your broken leg. You will say, "How cruel is he! He does not know how to touch." No, you will thank God that this man will help you. He may cause you some suffering (in the process) but after some time you will be healed.

Every pain that you cause to a man will come back to you.

All sufferings that you experience are for rectifying some infirmity that exists in you.

Man will be put to certain tests which he must pass. We should not be afraid of anything. When going through the greatest suffering, man must see the hand of God that acts within that given instance. You all must feel the presence of God to think that His hand is above you. And the scripture says, "Everything that happens to those who love God will turn for good!" I do not want us to go back. You have not finished your development. You will all pass through the way of Christ.

Our world is a world of suffering in the first place. Those angels from the invisible world who do not know what suffering is are sent to earth so they can learn what it is. That knowledge (about suffering) we must acquire by trial. Now whether we want them or not, these sufferings, they will come. But believe that you will never experience suffering that you cannot bear. Sufferings that are necessary for your development will come to you. Too big a suffering that you cannot bear will not come on you.

Divine is this that awakens in us the nicest thoughts, and the nicest feelings, and the nicest deeds.

Develop in you that faith which brings the power to the mind of man. Develop in you the hope that brings the power to the man's feelings. And develop love; first, develop love that itself brings the Divine life. And Christ says: "This is eternal life, to know God!"

Thought is that which regulates all feelings and puts them in harmony.

The scripture says, "Without faith, man cannot work." Without faith, love, and hope man can not work. If we do not have faith, hope, and love, we cannot work with God!

Put a pleasant thought in your mind. Do not think that you are a great sinner. Rather, think that you are a saint, even though you are not one. You are not a musician, but think that you are a great one. That you are not is OK. Think that you are musician. It is alright.

It is a law: you can deposit in yourself everything that is nice. And "nice" brings riches, strength, and power in man! Bring in the niceness into yourself without hesitation. Think that you have faith, even if you don't have it. Take up with somebody who has strong faith and start thinking that you also have such a faith. Do this to have success.

Remember this Divine Law: that which you give to people will be given back to you. You yourself determine your faith, and how much people will be giving you. You put your hand in your pocket: you have a note of 100 leva, (Bulgarian currency), then a coin of 10 leva, 5 leva, and 1 lev. You pick up 1 lev and give it to somebody. And to you 1 lev will be given. You give 10 leva and to you 10 leva will be given. You give 100; you will be given 100 leva. Give generously. Generously give, but not with an eye on what you will take. Be generous in your thoughts and feelings. When you see somebody, wish him to finish his school successfully. Wish him to sing. To all people who go out into the world, wish them the best from all of your heart and all of your mind! The law is very truthful. What you wish to other people, other people will wish to you, and God will wish to you. What you do not wish to other people, God won't wish to you. There are no exceptions! With whatever measurement you measure, the same will be measured to you. If you measure with the measurement of Love, to you with love will be measured. If you measure with the measurement of compassion, to you with compassion will be measured. There are no exceptions in this law!

Do you know what prayer is? It is the most beautiful language that exists in the world. To pray means to talk to God. In your prayer you may happen to use these words, "Lord, why did you forget me?" The Lord will tell you, "I forgot you because you became deaf. You didn't listen. I forgot you because you became hard-hearted. I forgot you because you became stubborn. I forgot you because you became headstrong, shrewish. I forgot you because you think bad thoughts!" In order for the Lord not to forget you, be kind like your Father is.

I say, "Now the essential is not in our personal lives." The ideal in the world is to fulfill the Will of God on Earth. There Will of God is reasonable. Let's finish one work as He wants! And when He passes by to say, "This work is finished!"

Act well because people may imitate you (by following your example.)

What is your benefit if you are young and do not study? And what is your benefit if you are old and do not apply what you have learned?

Man has come on Earth for three Divine reasons: to glorify the name of God, to serve the Kingdom of God, and to do the Will of God. For the one who understands, this is the meaning of life. For the one who does not, he will put his glory first instead of God's; instead of serving the Kingdom of God, he will fulfill his own wishes, and instead of fulfilling the Will of God he will fulfill his own will.

Remember, every man who strives to uplift himself at the same time helps the whole of humanity! Every man who does not want to uplift himself is causing the stumbling of the whole of humanity! So, the issue is: no one lives for himself alone. When you serve God, you serve the whole humanity. And when you do not serve Him, you stumble yourself.

You cannot be a smart man if you do not have love. You cannot be good man if you do not have love, you cannot be fair if you do not have love. Love is an essential factor inside the human soul.

If the mind is bright, if the heart is warm, and if the will is strong, the man is healthy.

On Earth we need the following principle: to give unto others that which you give to yourself.

If you do not want to fulfill the Will of God, if you do not want to do favors for others, you are alienating yourself from God. If you grumble, you are moving away from God. Be thankful in every moment with that which you have. What you have is a great good that God has given you. Be grateful with the life that you have now at this moment, because the whole of eternity, the whole future is yours.

If somebody insults you, give him a box of candy.

If a man wants to be perfect, he must not give way to the bad wishes in himself. He must exercise self-restraint.

Love is for the strongest people.

Let this be clear: until a man becomes good, fair, smart, loving, and until he loves Truth, he cannot be happy.

Man is loved for something essential inside of himself.

We have to constantly do the Will of God in our daily lives, not just in one particular moment, because our happiness depends upon the Will of God. God wants us to be happy. God does not want even one single man to be unhappy. But because we do not understand the Will of God, we first impose our will and then His. But the law is as follows: first apply God's Will, and after you apply that, then you can apply yours.

All of our difficulties are due to that fact that we expect things to happen without a lot of work. Work is something beautiful. Therein is what it means to work. In "work" I understand to love; then to love knowledge; then to love Truth. Whatever you study, know it well, not just a part or half of it.

Good rests in righteous love.

Love thus as God requires.

When you do good, do not expect a reward. Your reward will be the love that will be shown to you. .

In all things in life, see the nice side.

With your heart you connect with people, with your mind you are connected with the angels, but with your soul you are connected with God. The soul has come out of God. God breathed into man and he became the living soul. He made him in his image and likeness. And that soul which God has put in man He loves. He loves this Truth which He has deposited in you. This Truth rests in you. God has given you one excellent mind, excellent heart, and excellent soul. The mind and the heart are clothes of the soul, but the essential part of man is the soul which is the breath that has come out of God. You have to have an excellent mind and heart, so they can help your soul. But that which the mind and the heart acquire, is the good that will bring your blessings in the future.

Now do not get discouraged in life. Be persistent upon what you wish until your prayers are realized.

To love is doing God's work.

Love brings freedom. Freedom comes out of Love. When Love comes, then freedom comes. Love also brings knowledge.

You have to support the ideas of Love. You have to know that Love is the great creative principle. Everything in the world is created through Love. Do not want first to understand things before believing in them.

Music is a great Divine method which brings warmth into all brain centers. You cannot awaken your will without singing. You cannot awaken your love without singing. Your love can not show without singing. I consider talking as music.

This world is created through music.

First thing in the world is to organize your warmth. Let your heart be warm. In other words, strive to always throw out the discontent from your heart and to be content. Be content that you are on Earth.

If you know how to pronounce the word "Love" as it should be, the poor will get rich, the sick will become healthy, the weak will become strong, and the ignorant will become learned. The change won't come all at once, but gradually.

God loves the sinful people. God seeks the sinful people to uplift them.

Do not think that when you love in life you will lose. Man who loves does the Will of God. Man, who does not love, does not do the Will of God. This is a law. Do not feel sorry that you love.

Love is the right way for acquiring all of God's benefits. If you want to become a singer, deposit love in your efforts. Love will make you a singer, a learned man, a rich man, a beautiful man. Put love into it, and you won't be deprived from any benefits. This principle all of you have to try out.

Diseases come out for three reasons. There are diseases that come from the people's actions in the physical world, from the feelings world, and the third reason is from human thoughts. All nervous breakdowns that people have are due to their thoughts being out of harmony.

There is a saying: "Guard against the devil." No, the devil must guard against us. If you have to guard against the devil, you are fearful. But if the devil must guard against you, he is weak. If you have to guard against him, he is stronger than you. But if he is on guard against you, he is weaker than you. We are stronger than the devil, keep this in mind. Somewhere, though, he is a better master; he is a master of lies. When he comes, he makes a trap like the spiders do to catch a fly, but with slyness, not with strength.

The devil does his job very well. I like one trait of his -- he is very diligent; there is no being more diligent than he. If you kick him out through the door, he enters through the chimney. If you kick him out through the chimney, he will enter through some small hole. A hundred times you kick him out, he'll come back again. He will say, "Good afternoon, how are you?" He is very polite. He will praise you a lot. Anyone who praises a lot is a very little person. He will light you up from four sides and you will burn. He has something to take from you. When he comes, he will say, "You are genius. There is no being like you in the world. I have not seen anybody like you." And after he finishes his work with you he'll say, "I have not seen bigger fool than you." When the devil makes something wrong, he considers that as good. But when he makes something good, he considers it a mistake. And when he praises somebody, then he says: "For these praises I will rub his nose."

If you want to be smart - befriend smart people, not foolish people. Befriend the smartest people. If you want to be good - befriend the best people.

When you think about God, think how He is the smartest and noblest being.

Mathew 12:50
"For whoever does the Will of my Father in heaven is my brother and sister and mother."

That one who wants to be brother, and sister, and mother of Christ must be a first class hero in the world. A first class hero, not just in the general meaning, is a hero of mind, soul, and spirit. He must have a heart as pure as a crystal; he must have light in his mind as that of the sun; to have one lofty, noble, and vast soul like the whole universe; and a robust Spirit like God. This is what is required and which is necessary.

Great is God's Will. It will never change by any means. This is one mathematical problem which must be solved. Until you fulfill the will of this one-for-all Father who is up in Heaven, you cannot become a brother and sister of the great Master, Christ. Do you know what "Father" means? Father is the one who moves the world. God is that only one who puts everything in order.

To fulfill the Will of God is the loftiest and holiest height to which we can attain in this life.

All crimes must be perfectly swept out from our lives. When you clean up your world from all criminal affairs, bad thoughts and wishes, and project Divine Love through your soul and spirit, then you will become sister, brother, and mother. Then come to me and I myself will open the door of the Temple and will bring you inside. I am speaking to you clearly! From all of you what is wanted is for you to be heroes in the new teaching, and not cowards.

If you complain about your husband, you are not brother, sister and mother of Christ. If you cannot carry the smallest difficulties you are not yet brother, sister, and mother of Christ. But if you can endure everything, **you are close to the Temple, you will enter inside. Soon Christ will come, will unlock the door and say, "Enter the sanctuary, you are my brother, and sister and mother; you can be a disciple."**

First you have to be brother, sister and mother to fulfill God's will. Love must become a factor in your soul, heart, and spirit, and in that way to be realized and materialized, and then you will be before the door of the Temple to accept the new life of resurrection. Righteousness is one quality of the human soul. Every soul is born to be righteous, and at the beginning it was righteous. Acquire this quality - that inheritance of yours that is given to you - to be righteous. Every soul must be righteous. Why? So that from it can come out the great light, and when you have that righteousness and light, Love will show itself to you.

Somebody asks, "Am I a smart man?" If you think over great and lofty things and you can solve them, you are smart. But if you do not think over anything, you are a first class fool.

Christ says, "The righteous will shine in the Kingdom of the Father," i.e., in the Kingdom of Love. Which Father? He is the Father of Love. This is it. And this Love is the one that unites the whole universe, all beings from one side to the other in this great harmony of Love.

Do not misunderstand Love to mean softness. It is gentle, but not soft. Love is one great power so stable it never changes. Love is gentle.

To all those who oppose Love, for them is coming the most terrifying hell fire. And when they oppose it, they themselves create this fire of torment. They are tormented because they do not accept Love; and when they oppose it, they will become the unhappiest. But when they accept Love, they will become the happiest. For a man to accept Love he must be righteous, not like the contemporary people, but he must shine.

If you shine as I am telling you, you will be freed from all torment of the sly. This is not a philosophy of fear, but a great reality.

"The righteous will shine in the Kingdom of their Father. Whoever has ears to listen, let him listen."

The one who loves and the one, who does not, cannot both live in one place. I see that such a man, who does not love, does not have any love in his soul. Why he does not have love? It is because he thinks of and for himself only.

Your tongue must be golden; gold-plated must be your tongue. I mean a tongue causes words to leaven with Divine Wisdom, talking with reason, and no impure word must come out of your mouth. From your eyes, no bad look of lust or greed must come out. Those senses must be really pure. When you look upon somebody, he must feel joy; he must feel that his soul is uplifted. Love is a power which does not submit to any law. It will always tie you, but you can never tie it up, and with whatever ropes you tie it up, it is free, it melts down everything. This Love now enters these righteous souls so they can shine.

"Whoever has ears to hear, let him hear." Now, deposit Love like a fire that burns constantly. Or open your hearts for this Love, the Divine Love, I am not talking about the human love. This Love is the one soft fire, which when it enters, will bring peace in your spirit, light to your mind and strength in your hands and legs. It will remove all of your ailments and pains.

"Whoever has ears to hear, let him hear." Righteousness is the foundation upon which Love will manifest in the Future and will illuminate the human soul.

And so, remember the verse: "The righteous will shine in the Kingdom of their Father. Whoever has ears to hear, let him hear." This is the contemporary news of Christ, Who is talking to you now. This is His teaching. This Christ does not belong to the Orthodox Church, or to the Evangelical. This Christ is one in the world. There should be no double entendre on this. He is a Christ of Love, of the manifested Love in righteousness, which shines in those who love Him.

There are three important things in life. There is nothing more necessary than eating. Eating is the prerequisite of the physical life. Eating is the first introduction of Nature, the most necessary deed. But the most pleasant thing in the self-conscious life is music, singing. Music is the introduction of man's mental life. But the greatest in the world this is prayer. Consequently, the most necessary is eating, the most pleasant is music, but the greatest is prayer, which connects us with God – the Eternal, Who gives us meaning from inside. Prayer is the introduction of the Divine world. So there are three introductions into the world: introduction of eating, music, and prayer. Somebody may ask: "Why should we pray?" You will read this introduction so you can understand the inner meaning of the supernatural life.

Now John says, "Because God so much loved the world, he gave His only son, so that no one dies who believes in Him, but has eternal life."

The son – is the higher reason. He is the Divine Wisdom in which man must believe. The reasonable life is what man must believe in, accept, and apply.

Now for God to love the world there had to be something in this world. What will He love in the world? In the world are all those spirits that have come out of Him. And He sent His Love so that people can believe and thereby apply that principle so they can have an eternal life. This is the Divine wish -- to make all immortal like Him. But this immortality is not given from outside. John says, "You have to believe in His son, Who is the manifestation of the whole Divine Wisdom, which is hidden in Him. This you cannot understand, yet when one soul comes to know this Wisdom they will acquire eternal life as a reward.

If marrying becomes a reason not to find truth in life, do not marry. But if it becomes a reason to find Truth, Love, and Wisdom, then I'll advise you to marry. Man or woman, most all of you marry. But if marrying becomes an obstacle to being free, do not marry! "But what will happen to the world?" Whatever may happen with this world, let it happen! We will make another, new world with different laws. You cannot have it both ways, (both the old and the new ways at once.) We have to have one defined philosophy. Every thing that stops us from finding that great Love, that stops our consciousness from becoming Divine, and attaining God's Wisdom -- all these stumbling blocks must be removed right away.

Life will come only with Love!

Our goal here on Earth is eternal life -- to attain those conditions by which we can study Love and Wisdom.

Now in you must be born the new consciousness to serve God with Love. Every action of yours must be a loving act, acts in which you must put all your life, all your thoughts, mind, will and heart. And everything you do, do it like you are doing it for God only. And consequently, when you fulfill such an act, you can be pleased that you did it with Love. And the more you give, the more will come from above.

Prayer is the greatest thing. I am talking about an experienced action, and I have tried it. And there is nothing greater in my soul than prayer; there is nothing more pleasant than music, and nothing more necessary than eating. These are real experiences and verified truths.
There is a saying, "The good and evil will come back to their spring." Everything that you think will first come back to you, and then goes to others.

Do you know what it means to be calm? To be calm means no matter what you are told, neither your eyes nor your heart should waiver. Do not cry like the others, if your husband dies. Simply say, "That is the will of God."

And so, the disciples must change their ways of life. They must think that the Lord lives in them. Which Lord? The Lord of Love, and always, even in the worst situation they are not allowed to complain, but on the contrary, to thank God for everything.

The disciple is not allowed to ever forget the Lord. Never!

But the one who loves the Lord must love all people because of the Lord, and must be patient with all. As is the Lord, so you must be.

Be heroes, be content. Be unusual people, talented in the first degree in Wisdom, Love, and Truth, in all your manifestations, in all your life. This is what Christ wants from his disciples. Be unusual.

There is God, because Love exists in the world.

The hero is that one who is ready to die for one lofty idea.

If we talk about Truth and lies, we have to define them as two quantities. How can Truth and lies be distinguished from each other? When Truth enters man, it gives an element of bravery to him. When he knows the truth of some idea, he is ready to die for it. But when a lie enters man, it makes him fearful. Everything that makes man fearful contains something false or some lie in it. But everything that makes man brave and determined, that makes him think and reason, brings him close to the Truth. That is how things are in practicality. Does what I am speaking make you fearful? If it makes you fearful, I am telling you a lie. But if what I tell you makes you brave, determined, and happy in life, then I am speaking the truth.

Lies destroy, but Truth builds.

You want to become disciples – then the Will of God; the God's Love must permeate your souls such that you become brothers, sisters and mothers of Christ. A disciple can become only he who is a brother, a sister, and mother in accordance with the great Divine Law.

He who wants to be a disciple like an occultist, or a mystic, or brother of humanity, must have Love in his soul as the driving principle, and must take all sacrifices in stride. Now you will ask me "Can that be?" It can. No coercion is necessary to use.

Love gives and takes by the law of freedom, but not by force. You, when you give, must not be sorry. And when you take again you must not be sorry. Give everything and take everything; this is according to the great Divine Law. But contemporary people give little, yet take everything. That is the moral of present day humanity.

When someone is invited to become a disciple, he must not say, "Wait; let me think a little bit."

It is a great thing to be a Christian disciple. The disciple must be of high morality, which under no circumstance and before no difficulties should retreat. Also, because of no other power in this world should this morality be broken. The disciple must endure everything! You may say, "Can that be?" It can.

Life is a puzzle, a great and pleasant puzzle for solving. And again I will tell you that in order to solve life; you have to put Love as the foundation. In order to solve the puzzle correctly, begin with Love, then Wisdom will come to your aid, and lastly comes Truth. Thus, when those three great principles come into your life, you will be able to solve this great puzzle.

We have to ennoble our thoughts, feelings, wishes and actions. But we should not do this all at once. I do not mean this work that we do now to be finished all at once.

The first principle for the disciple is to become brother and sister and mother of Christ. God's Love must fill your heart, soul, and spirit, and then you will become brother, sister, and mother. And after you apply this principle, you will be a disciple.

To be brothers, and sisters, and mother of Christ is the greatest attainment for us. Did you become brother, sister, and mother of Christ? You didn't? Then you need to put all of your efforts to become one.

Now, God is Love, but you must be Love also. A loving person with another Loving person understands one another. A wise person with another wise person understands one another, a righteous person with another righteous person understands one another, a truthful person with truthful person, and a person of virtue with another person of virtue understands one another. That's how things are. Love and you will be loved, think about others and others will think about you, illuminate and you will be illuminated. This is how the great law in nature works.

The scripture says, "Fear of God is a foundation of Wisdom." Consequently, dread only God. Have fear only of God, but do not fear anything else. Any other fear will bring sin to you. We will accept fear in only one case, which is of God. In any other case there should be no fear!

In place of lies, we will bring truth. Instead of the negative, we will seek the positive in things. Do not think about lies, think about the Truth.

You will say, "In our home must reign full Truth without any lies; full Love without any hatred; full Wisdom, full Righteousness, and full Goodness. We have decided to serve God without any exception! We will not twist our soul for any one!"

Love all people without any exceptions. Your soul must be filled with Love.

The love that is in me is God.

Let the words that come out of your mouth be sweet like honey, and as crystal fresh as dew.

When you dip into the Divine Love and feel all of its vibrations, when you understand this Love, then you will understand the symphony of this life. As of now you appreciate life only from your point of view.

We have to have pure souls and bright minds, and not put our trust and hopes in the banks. It is a corruption to do so. You create money for facilitation, not to trust in. And consequently we must not deposit money in the banks, but to become living banks of God. That energy that God has put in us we have to use only for good.

"Whoever eats my flesh and drinks my blood will have an eternal life and I will resurrect him in the last day." John 6:54

"If you do not eat from this flesh and do not drink from my blood you will not have an eternal life," i.e., if you do not accept my teaching and do not apply it, you can not acquire eternal life.

There is no greater poison in the world than human egoism.

Your heart must be opened only for God and nobody else.

Unite with Love and split with the world and you will be free.

"And in the last day I will resurrect him," means that those who "drink my blood and eat my flesh" understand the law of uniting with God and splitting with the world.

There is no one more blessed - says Christ - than the one who listens to the word of God and fulfils it. The word of God this is the greatest in the world. I would translate it to your language. This expression "the Word of God" is incomprehensible; yet you have read it over and over many times. What does it mean "the Word of God?" It is that primary moment, when the Divine Love consciously manifested itself in the material world.

The Lord lives in your soul, not in your body.

The greatest law in the spiritual world is that we have to put our mind to work with all of its strengths.

Our mind is then only good when it arranges our affairs well, comprehends them well, transmits them well, and does not twist the facts so that people can see them well.

If you got angered, your mind and your heart are not in their right places.

If you are unhappy, you have not put your mind to work and as a result you cannot achieve anything. Put it to work and you will see what a great job it can do for you.

The mind and the heart must be put to work. How? The heart is created to love, the mind to think. If you do not think.- then your mind is not there. If you do not love.- then your heart is not there.

Christ says: "More blessed is he who listens to the Word of God and keeps it." He has said many more things, but they were not written. He has set laws and rules for His disciples on how to live. And in all my lectures I have a goal to get you to think and to love.

The reasonable man is that one who provides his wife with all conditions she need to grow and develop, and does not tell her even one bad word nor sends her even one bad look. And the reasonable woman is that one who appreciates her husband, and gives him all conditions so he can show his love and his noble and lofty thoughts.

If somebody says, "I hate you," the word "hate" for me is excellent. Why? Because hatred reminds me of Love. Consequently, when he hates, I'll thank him for reminding me about Love. When he says, "You lie," I think about the Truth. Or if someone says, "You are a fool," I am glad, and begin to think about Wisdom. I do a permutation of the energies. This is what reason is.

The first thing that you must keep is these minds of yours -- put them to work and do not criticize anyone. If you want to develop your mind, your mind must not be like a worm (buried in the dirt.) In you, in your soul, you must be as lenient with people as you are toward yourself. Think of others as you think for yourself. This is the right thing to do. If I put myself higher, but you lower, this is not a natural situation.

Christ says, "More blessed is the one who listens and keeps the word of God." The mind and the heart must understand this Word of God. You all can now apply this law.

One day the Bulgarians will come to know that I was a great friend of theirs. When I depart I do not want any monuments and if they make me any I will destroy them. Love wants God all (people) to love one another like brothers and sisters these are the monuments of the future. In the head of every priest, preacher, teacher, and mother this must be imprinted: **brotherhood and sisterhood is needed in the world.**

Do not expect to be a professor or a famous person; those are secondary things. Look to become a true man loved by God, and you shall love Him. Know all your brothers and sisters, love them and be ready to sacrifice yourself for them.

Love does not enslave.

My teaching is a teaching of Love, brotherhood and sisterhood of absolute freedom in which everyone respects the rights of the others. And the powerful are ready to be servants of the little and weak. This is the Divine teaching, this is what Christ has said and this is what Christ who is coming from above will tell you.

Love is a work, a serious work. Serious work is wanted from us. And when you meet someone do not discriminate. Often when I pass by I see how difficult it is for us to keep one and the same attitude towards all (people). When you meet rich and poor, love them equally. Do not differentiate. Have equal disposition of your spirit to both of them, without having any hatred in your heart. Tomorrow if this rich man comes in need, give him help the same as you could give to the poor one. Nurture equal disposition in yourself toward all--this is what is required now from the new culture.

When you want to get into a quarrel with someone, do not utilize knowledge of how to quarrel, be foolish in that moment. But when you want to do something good, (a good deed), that is the time to be very smart man.

The eyes always must express the Divine Truth, and the only thing in us that never lies are the eyes. The eyes must show the Divine Truth.

It is hard for man to speak the Truth.

If our teaching does not uplift us, if we in this life cannot set right firstly our organisms, then our feelings, and thoughts, it means we have lived in vain. Our souls are excellent. I am not referring to them.

If Christ comes today in the first place He will preach Love, brotherhood and equality. Why? -- Because now the human evolution requires it. This law is necessary now.

There is no other power that can connect people, not to unite them, but to make them comrades, to reconcile them, like Love. But not that love of the senses, that love is not enough; not that temporary mood, it is not Love. Love is one conscious power which can always warm you up and take down the burden of your heart. Love won't keep you hungry: Love is that power which gives people all goodness. It is an inner aspiration.

Whoever knows the God of Love; he revives and comes back to life. For him, life attains full meaning, and he becomes a citizen of the Great Kingdom in the material and spiritual world.

We should be not pastors, priests, or professors, but we all have to become servants; servants of the great Lord of Love. Do you understand? We all have to become servants – men, women, and children.

There is no historical Christ, there is no cosmic Christ, but there is one living Christ of Love, Who lives now in our souls – in every noble motive inside our souls. This one is the living Christ, (the love, and the noble motive). Whether He is in the heart of a simple man, or a judge, or a poor man, or an animal – it is the same.

If anything is done in the name of Love and Wisdom, there is no crime in it. When we apply God's Love and God is in us, when I am in God and God in me, and He finishes a certain job, then man is uplifted. Temptations will come: but without God and without Love it is the worst. But with God and with Love we will do the best deeds.
God can do anything. But without Love we will do the worst deeds; with Love, the best. And all must think like that.

Let's deposit this great principle of "Love."
"It is difficult, it is very difficult." I know that it is. It is one of the hardest tests to let Love in your heart.

The human soul is noble. And this soul is in the condition to get uplifted and to transform; and in one minute to become like a diamond. The sinner can in one minute become righteous, but an absolute decision is needed from him. We can live for God, but for which God? – The God of Love.

This Word must be spread around the world; but not by the old law, but by the new one – the law of Love.

You say, "Some things are possible, some impossible." I say that for Love everything is possible. How is that possible? If you can love all people everything is possible. Not to love as of up to now, no, no; this feeling (of Love) is the loftiest, the noblest, which from now on must be developed in the human soul. The feeling of Love has not begun to develop in you yet. When that feeling shows in the human soul – I call it **insight** – man receives such powers that he reconciles with everything. And in everything he sees no evil, not only he sees no evil, but he is a master – he can turn all things into good.

Now we shake hands only with the right hand, but when we love someone, we must shake hands with both hands. Now we do it aristocratically – with one hand. Whoever we love, we have to hold with both hands to convey the Wisdom and the Love. The Divine must be given and passed around everywhere.

From all of you I want two things by which to distinguish yourselves: be people of Love and Wisdom. He who does not carry these two great laws of Love and Wisdom cannot be from the new teaching.

Sacrifice is only a law of atonement of our sins. When a man loses his purity, he can restore it only through the law of sacrifice. Sacrifice is only a law of restoration of our primary purity. And after we attain our purity we will have a foundation from which to see God. And when we see God we will attain the true consciousness for our development.

And so with sacrifice is attained purity. With purity is established the foundation to see God. And with seeing God begins the true conscious, the true development, the evolution of the soul and its life. Consequently, when we say that we have to love, I understand that to say that we have to begin to live.

The heart this is the conscious life. The mind this is the self-conscious life. The soul is the subconscious life and the power of the spirit. This is the super conscious life.

In Love there is no groaning, no difficulties, no insanity or madness. There is no loss of strength; there is no death. There is a great life inside Love.

When man studies Love, the greatest heroism is required from him.

When man sacrifices himself for others, he has already uplifted himself one step higher.

You have to feel yourselves like souls. You should never accept, from whoever it may be, a sacrifice for yourself. No master, whoever he could be, wants sacrifices from his disciples for himself. If the disciple wants, on his own, to sacrifice himself for his own self-perfection to attain his original purity, then he can do it. But the master does not need his sacrifice.

The work that we do now in our lives will have a relationship to our future lives.

The one who steals masterfully will also be as crafty in his other affairs. He who hates a lot can love a lot too. When I see some bad man in the world, I am glad for him, because when this man comes to know the truth, he will be again as covetous of the good as he was of the evil.

Whatever Christ has spoken, that is the teaching with its basic principles that can be applied right now. It will be the same even after thousands and millions of years. Love until the end of the century and after it ends will be the same. When I say the same Love, I understand the same Love as substance and essence, not as form.

Every thought that makes man ready for self-sacrifice is a Divine one. There are no exceptions in this. Accept it; it comes from Christ. If you stop and begin wondering whether it is from that Christ Who lived 2,000 years ago, you lose everything.

I am not preaching to you about the crucified Christ. I am preaching to you about that Christ's resurrection of God's Love, God's Wisdom, God's Truth, Righteousness, and Virtue; and about that Christ Who brings life in Himself, Who brings Wisdom, knowledge to the world; of that Christ who brings Truth, Who comes to give us this inner light, to organize our homes, to give us Righteousness and with its measurement to measure and give us Virtue.

God can not be profaned. There must be no lies in His name. If I in the name of Christ mislead you, heavy will be the karma of this nation. No one can do well who has lied. Somebody says, "It is worth lying." No, never! Sometimes you can economize the truth, you can avoid the answer or you can keep quiet, but never tell a lie. If you can not say the truth – be quiet; if you can not say the truth – run; no one is forcing you to speak.

Luke 7:45
"You didn't give Me a kiss, but she since I came in has not stopped to kiss My feet."
The woman preferred to kiss the dusty feet of Christ, but not the clean ones of that of the bourgeois, because Christ was walking with sandals made from skin, without socks, and with bare feet. His legs were dusty. So, that woman didn't kiss Simon's feet, but those of Christ. "She says, "Lord you are dusty and unclean; me too. I will wash your feet, but You – wash my heart." And Christ replied: "It is said and done." (Note: The woman found the real thing in her life--God in Christ, and she did what a true disciple was supposed to do--become a servant to the Lord with all of her heart and soul. Jesus Christ's feet were dusty, and she did her very best to make them clean; with her tears she was washing them. She had a great faith in Christ.)

There should be no carrying around of offering plates in the church. That is a disgrace! All that must be thrown out. This is what Christ says.

Out go you who sold the name of Christ, and come only to serve for money, to collect it in your baskets. Christ didn't die for money. Christ came to serve in the name of God's Love and Wisdom, to resurrect the people. This is not just about our priests and pastors. When I speak the truth I say it in the name of Christ. Woe be to those who oppose these Divine truths. In Christ name, in the Divine name there are no any delusions.

When we love the people, we have come from God; but when we do not love them, from the devil.

First thing: When Christ comes into your home, you will wash His feet with your mouth. This translated into your language means, "You will serve Him with Wisdom and Love, and you will carry His word without any admixture that is a kiss. If you can serve Christ like that He will tell you, "Your sins are forgiven, and your names are being written in Heaven before the angels, and in the future you will become citizens of this Great Kingdom."

And teachers and everyone else must serve Christ with Love and Wisdom.

Now I preach to you not like to Bulgarians, or as to English, or as to French. I preach to you as you are like my brothers and sisters, like friends, like disciples, whom I hold on an equal level with me. I am giving you my best thoughts, although these people are shaking in the cold. (The master gave this lecture on 01/08/1922 in Sofia, Bulgaria. The saloon couldn't hold everyone so some of his followers were listening from outside through the open windows.) I am giving you the best of myself, I am acquainting you with these truths about which no one from 2,000 years ago has spoken. Why? – Because I love God, because I serve Him with Love and Wisdom. And you can all serve Him. You can all serve God with Love and Wisdom. We can all be brothers, with no difference of what is our level of development. We will go to work according to our strengths and abilities.

And so, serve with Love, serve with Wisdom. This teaching must be applied. In it is the power and the salvation in the future.

May my Lord give light, may He give you His Wisdom, and may He give you His knowledge to shine. This Lord of Love whom I serve, this Lord of Wisdom, Lord of Truth, may He give you all His blessings to know Him, in order to understand the deep meaning of this life, which you don't know yet. But be not just Bulgarians -- I wish you to be daughters and sons of this Lord, who has created the whole universe, to give you access to His kingdom to walk freely. I wish you to be worthy of His Love, to thank Him and to glorify Him. This is what I wish to all of you! May the Lord bless all of you with the greatest blessing, to give strength and bravery to all of you. And I believe that you will be heroes of the new culture of Love, the future new humanity, which bears the sign: **Love for all!**

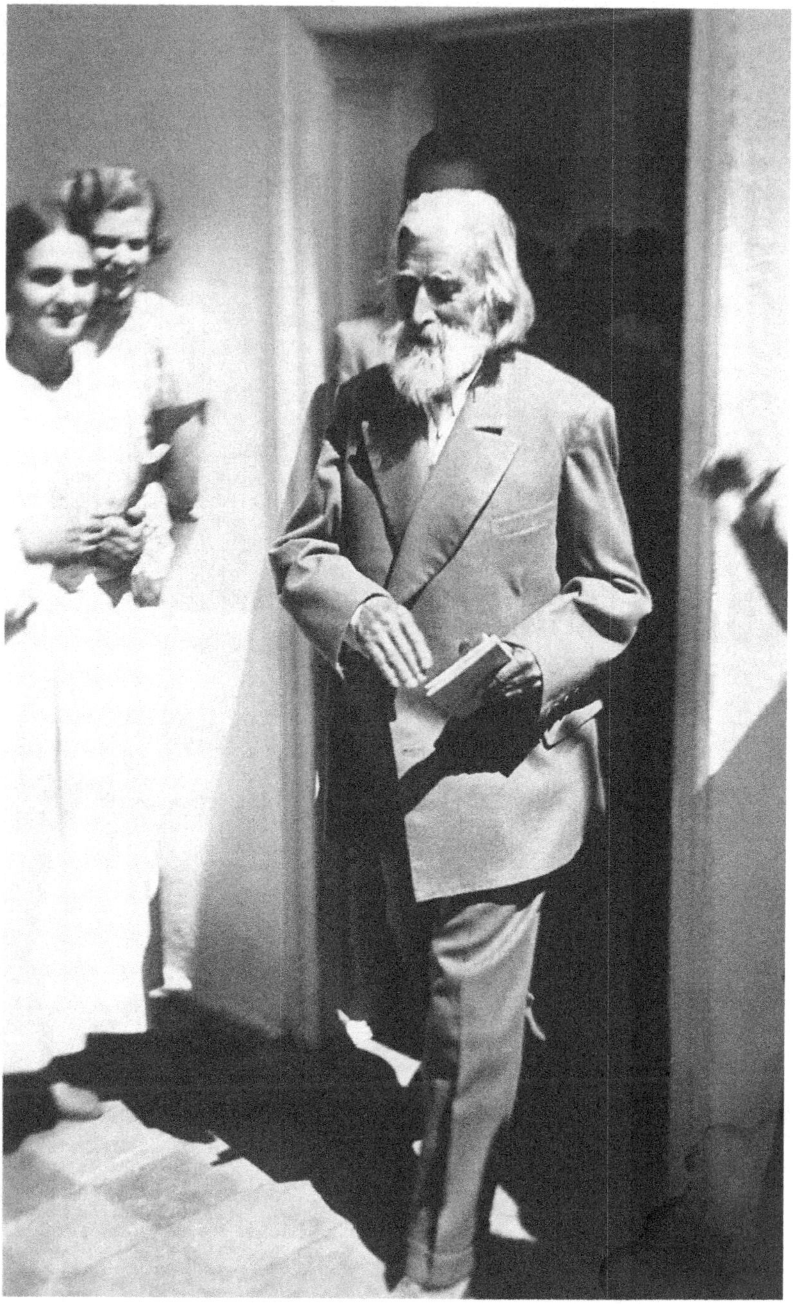

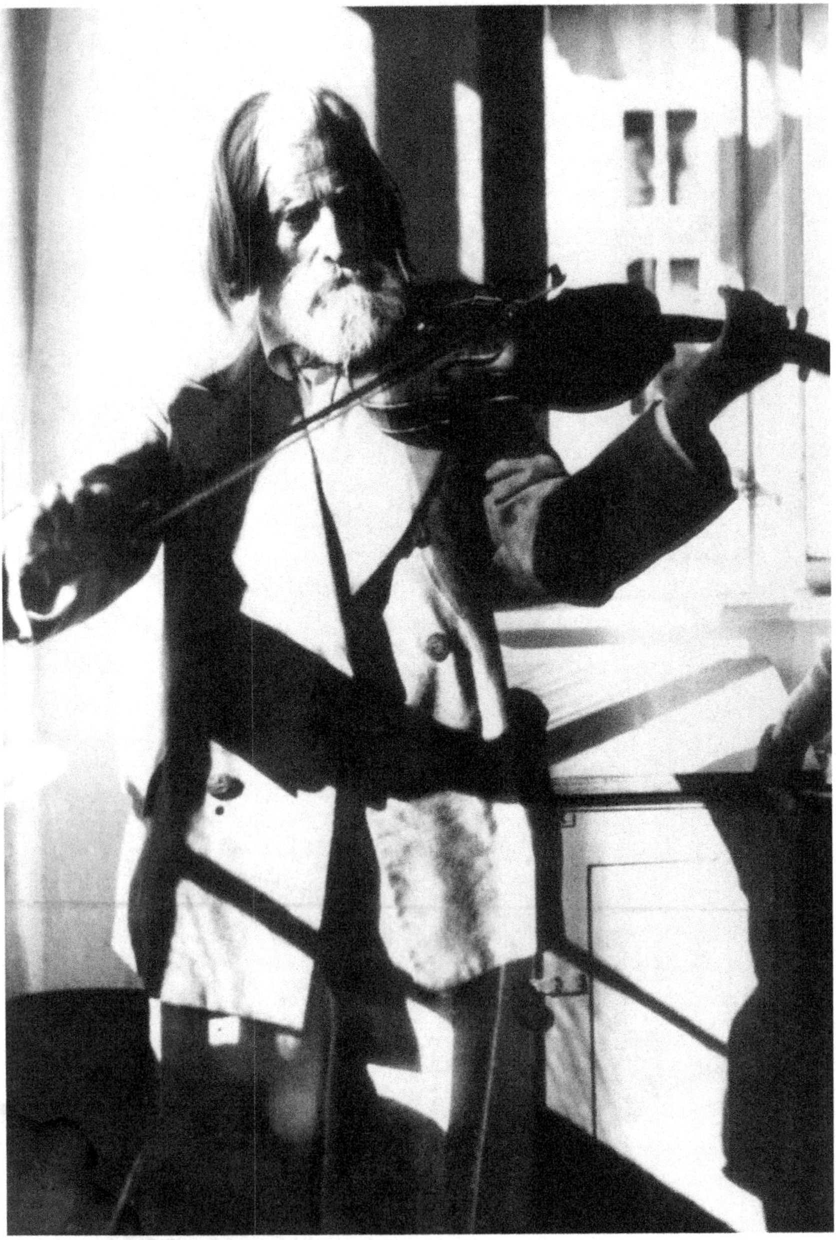

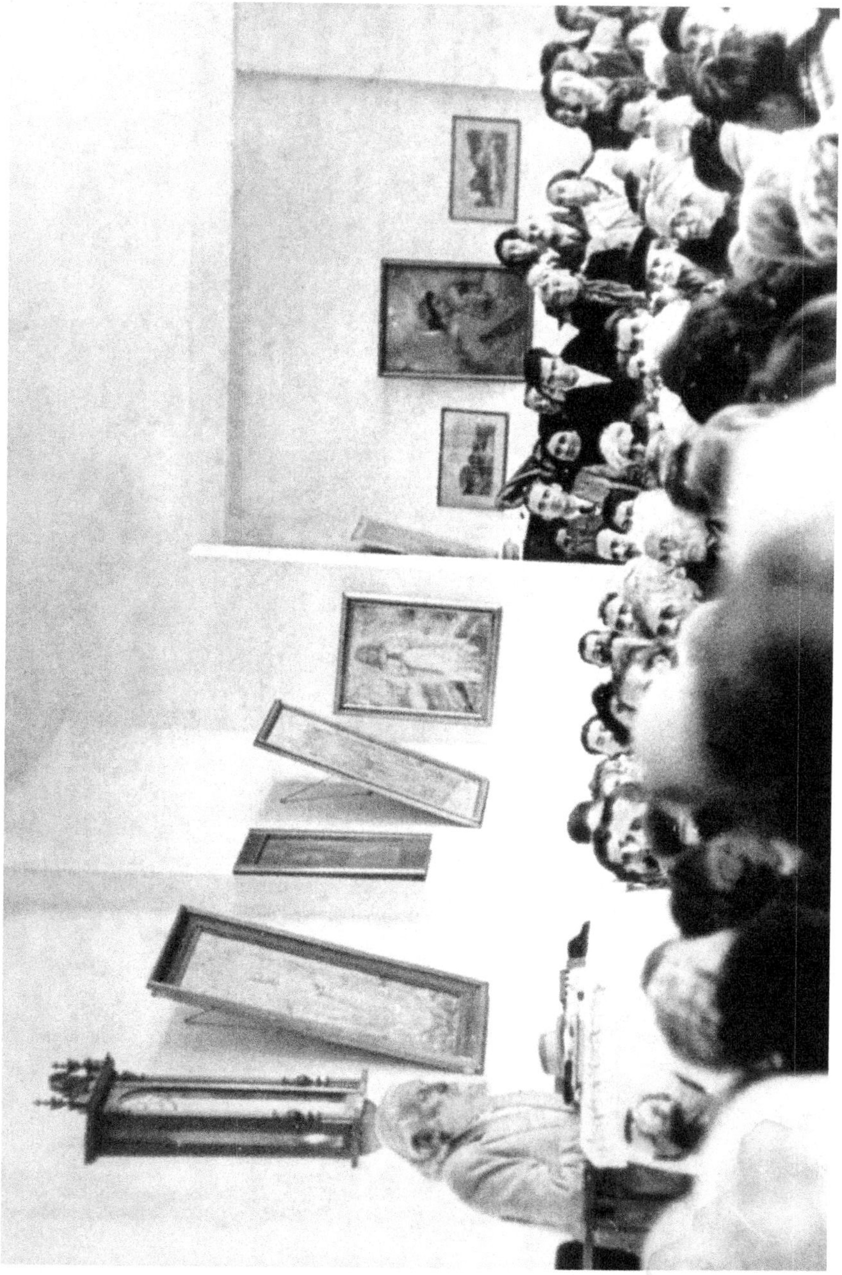

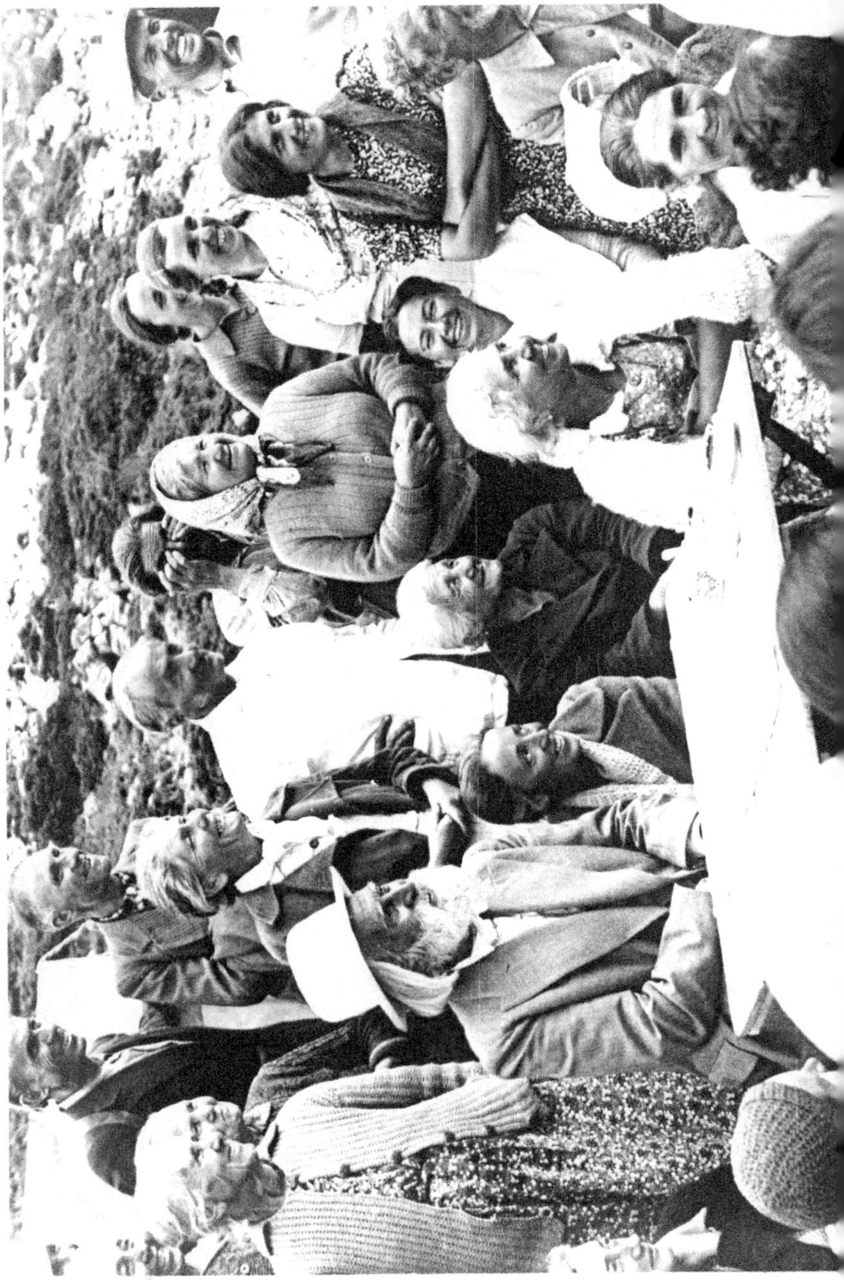

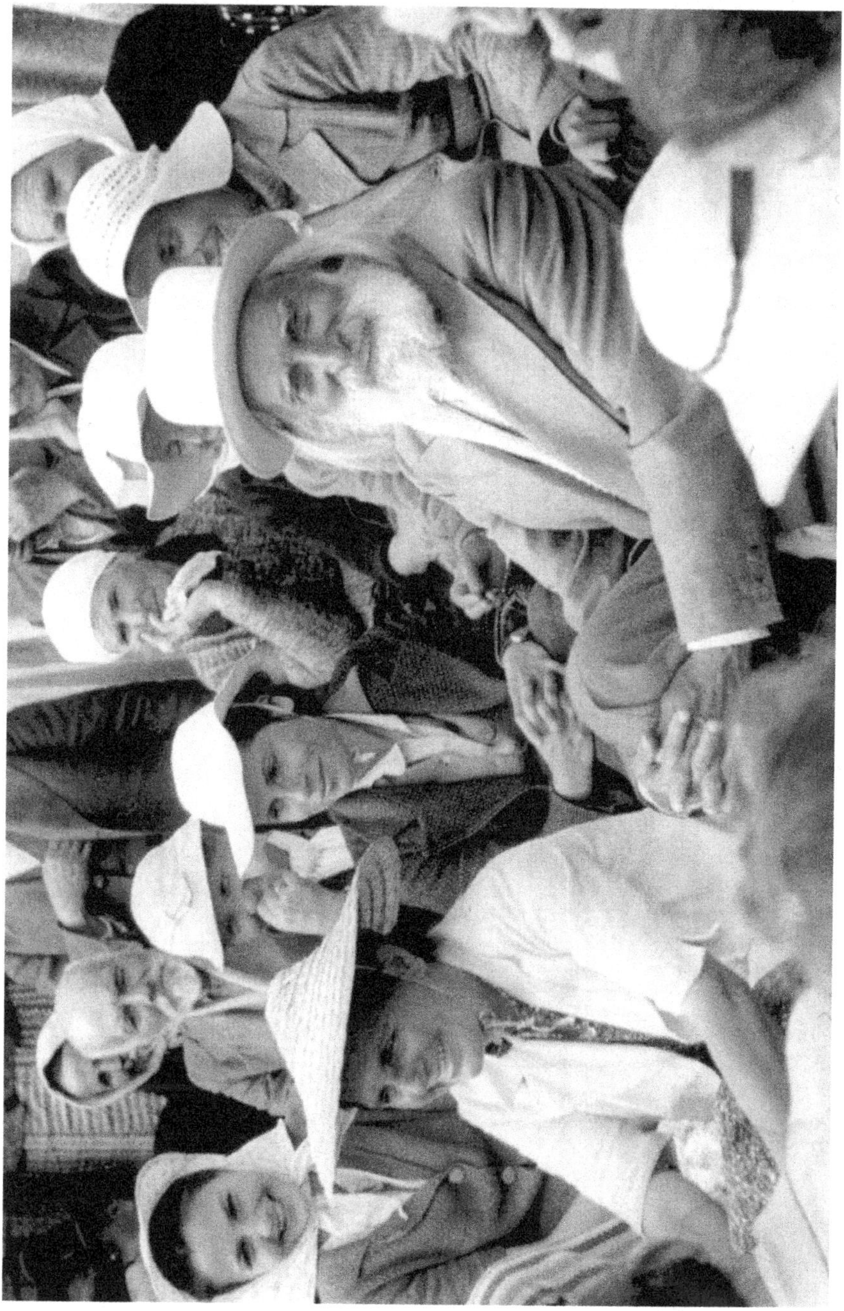

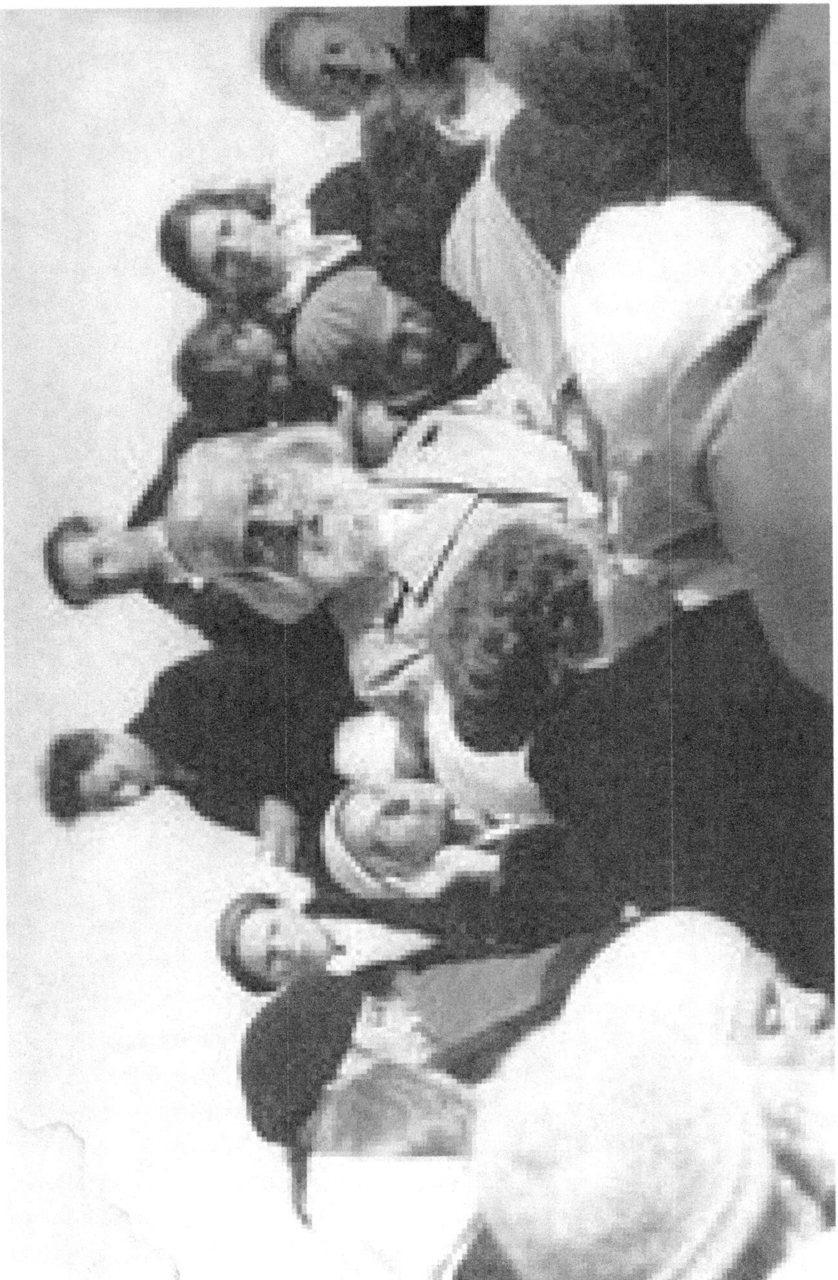

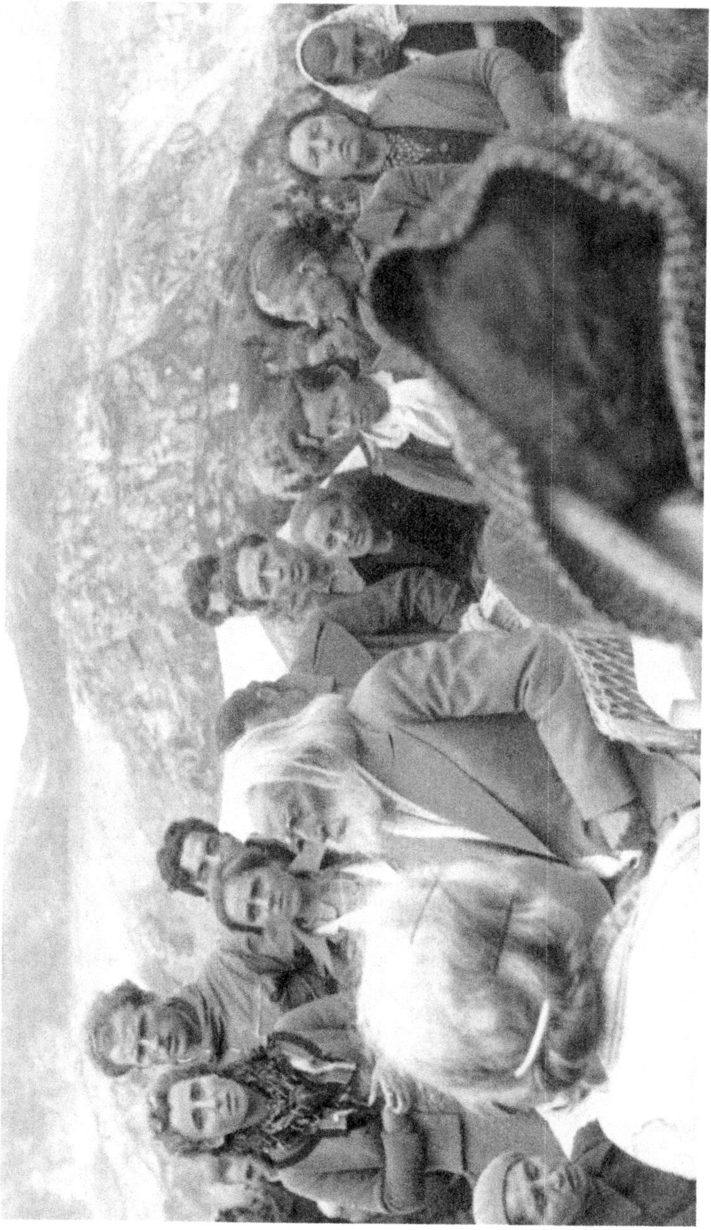

202

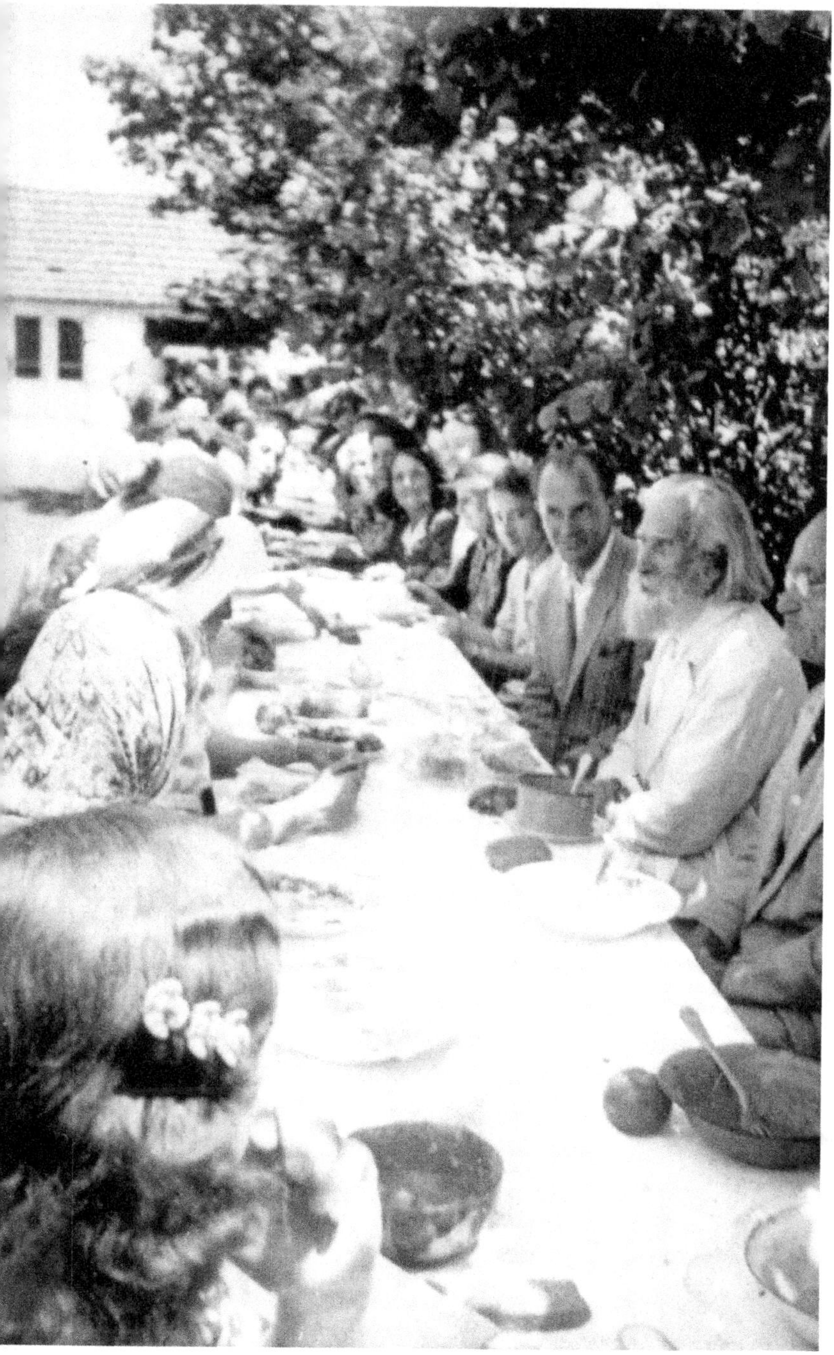

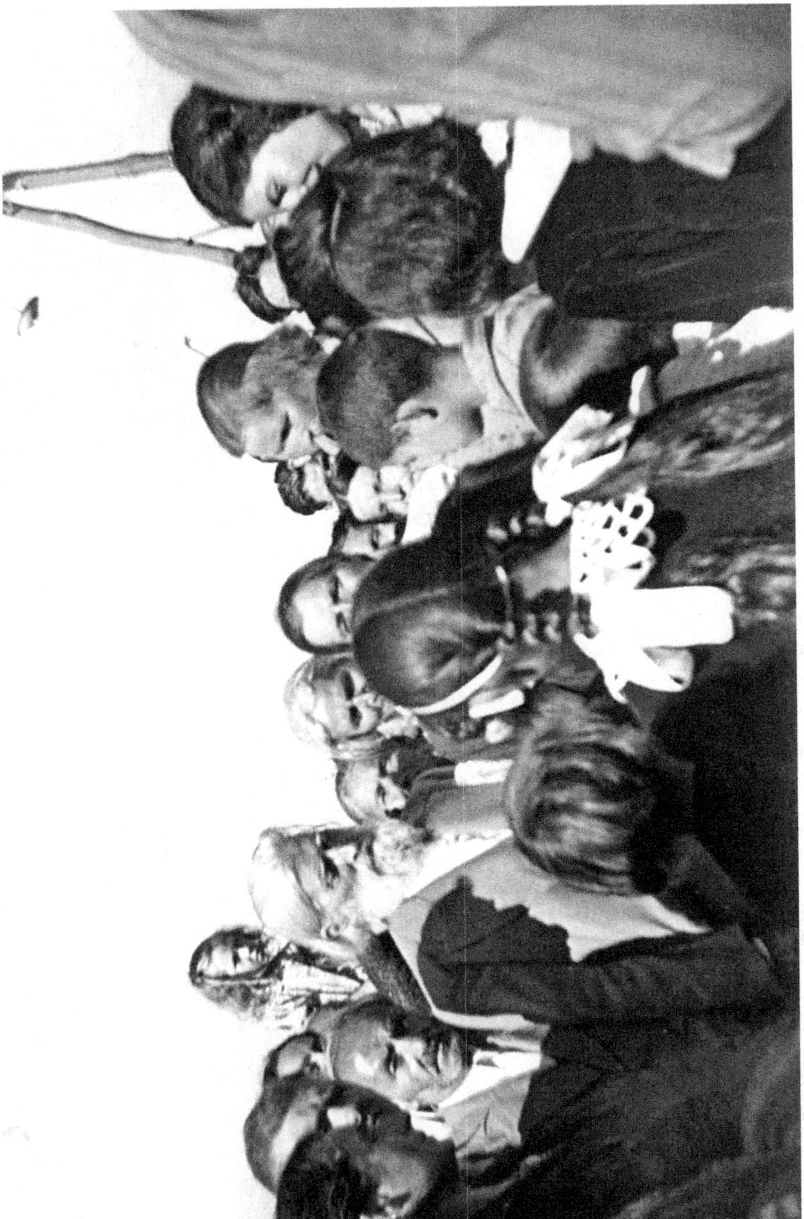

205

You cannot be a smart man if you do not have love.
You cannot be good man if you do not have love.
You cannot be fair if you do not have love.
Love is an essential factor inside the human soul.

Man must be three things: good, reasonable, and loving.

Made in the USA
Las Vegas, NV
09 April 2022